The ALASKA ADVENTURES
of a **NORWEGIAN CHEECHAKO**
a Greenhorn With A Gold Pan

May 30, 2010

To Carlyle
Happy 80th!

Love,
Edie Gilbertson

The ALASKA ADVENTURES
of a **NORWEGIAN CHEECHAKO**

a Greenhorn With A Gold Pan

HARALD EIDE

ALASKA NORTHWEST PUBLISHING COMPANY
Anchorage, Alaska

Design and Illustration by Warren D. Ernst
Alaska Northwest Publishing Company

Library of Congress Cataloging in Publication Data

Eide, Harald, 1896-
  The Alaska adventures of a Norwegian cheechako.

  Autobiographical.
  1. Alaska—Gold discoveries. 2. Frontier and
pioneer life—Alaska. 3. Eide, Harald, 1896-
I. Title.
F909.E34   979.8'04'0924   75-23014
ISBN 0-88240-063-0

Dedicated to Jewell

Contents

My New World 1

On a sunny morning in May, shortly after the turn of the century, I found myself in New York City. An immigrant, just off the ship, with my "old-country" suitcase in one hand and a bundle wrapped in newspapers under my arm containing all my earthly belongings, I made my way up Broadway in a daze of excitement at the wonders of America unfolding all about me.

I had come from a little fishing village in northern Norway where we had neither trains nor automobiles, our chief attraction being that of watching the triweekly ship arrive with mail and passengers from the southern part of the country. This startling change made me feel as if I had left one world behind me with a curtain drawn upon the past. The new world I had entered into so suddenly was almost too fantastic to grasp. I stopped frequently on my way to gawk up at the tall buildings that seemed to reach up into the blue canopy of the sky.

The street itself was a bedlam of noisy, endless traffic moving along like the tide of the sea. Streetcars clanged, with brakes squealing at every stop. Horses drawing wagons with freight and express plodded along in the morning heat. Ice wagons and pushcarts, snuggling close to the curb as they made deliveries, added to the confusion. Shining hansom cabs with silk-hatted drivers high on the seat dodged in and out of the traffic at a smart pace, flicking their whips over the horses' backs with a snappy, "Getty up, getty up!"

What fascinated me most in this maelstrom of transportation were the motorcars, or as some people called them, automobiles. They wove their way past swearing drivers trying to keep their balking horses in check until the smoky, noisy contraptions passed, leaving behind them a stinking bluish haze. Each time one of the motorcars appeared I would set my suitcase down on the sidewalk to watch the latest mechanical creation of American genius go by.

The driver of the thing was dressed in protective togs befitting a man in such a hazardous occupation. On his head he wore a large visored cap, the eyes protected with heavy goggles, and covering his hands as they gripped the steering wheel were leather gauntlets that came halfway to his elbows. It was a sight to behold, and right there I made up my mind that some day when I became rich in this new land I would buy me one of those horseless carriages and learn to drive it myself.

Many immigrants arriving in New York City had some relative or friend to meet them at the boat and get them started with a place to stay and some help in finding a job. Not so with me. I knew no one in America, but then I was very independent, both of spirit and pocketbook. I had been a member of

the American-Norwegian Arctic Expedition on Spitsbergen Island the previous 16 months and had saved my money. I was now, as Americans say, pretty well fixed.

Plodding along at a steady pace I reached 42nd Street about noon. Here on the shady side of the Times Building I sat on my suitcase to rest and cool off a bit, for it had been a long journey in the hot sun from down on the Battery where I landed. To make it worse I was still wearing my hot old-country underwear that by this time stuck to me like plaster. The sidewalk was full of people rushing about but no one paid any attention to me sitting there, wiping sweat from my face while surveying my surroundings.

An old man pushing an applecart stopped in front of me and said something in English that I couldn't understand. My English vocabulary consisted only of three words, "yes," "no" and "thank

2

you." But being hungry I held out a dime and the man handed me a big red apple and some change. I had made my first purchase in America.

While I was eating my apple a policeman came sauntering by, swinging his billy club back and forth. Stopping for a moment, he looked down on me. A hulk of a man, he was dressed in a heavy blue uniform that looked much too warm for this time of the year. Drops of perspiration streaked down his ruddy face under a helmet that seemed to rest on a pair of oversized ears. He said nothing to me, but satisfied I was not a crook nor breaking the law, he went on his way muttering to himself something that sounded like "greenhorn."

The long walk up Broadway had been so exciting that I hadn't given much thought to a place to stay, but by this time I was feeling badly in need of a bath and I was pleased to see a "Hotel" sign on a large building about half a block up the street. The word, hotel, is the same in English as it is in Norwegian so I recognized it on sight.

I had to cross the busy street, however, to get to the place. I gathered up my belongings and walked over to the edge of the curbstone, ready to tackle the adventure of crossing Broadway traffic. After several bad starts I finally made it, with the suitcase and bundle and with my coattail sticking straight out behind me, much to the amusement of some loafers on the curbside.

Timidly I entered the elegant lobby of the hotel where a crowd of people were sitting around in their Sunday clothes. A young fellow in uniform grabbed my suitcase and guided me up to the desk where an oily haired gent handed me a pen to sign my name. Now I was not particular at all, but the place turned out to be the Astor Hotel, one I had read about at some time or other in the newspapers back in the old country.

The ride up the elevator to my room was a bit frightening. I had never ridden in one before, but the man running the thing gave me a reassuring smile so I smiled back nonchalantly as if I had been going up and down in elevators all my life.

The elegance of my room nearly took my breath away. I gazed from the gilded light that hung on a chain from the ceiling to the pale blue rug on the floor. Among other things, I noticed a big overstuffed chair that nearly swallowed me up like Jonah's whale when I sat in it. The comforts of these rich Americans, I thought, leaning back into the chair and relaxing for the first time since leaving the ship in the early morning. It was almost too wonderful to be true, but here I was, a Norwegian, young and independent on his first day in America.

3

Getting hungrier by the minute, I set about to clean up a bit but found there was no washbasin in the room and I surely needed a bath after two weeks on the journey. Exploring further, I discovered a smaller room hanging onto the big one, with a bathtub and things inside. It was the first bathroom I had ever seen. Back in Norway we used to take our Saturday night baths in an iron tub in the middle of the kitchen floor. It was a bit chilly at times, especially when someone would walk through and leave the door open, but we didn't mind so much. Now the toilet inside the house—that, I'm sure, would have shocked the good burghers of my hometown. It was unheard of where I came from, back in those days.

Sitting down on the edge of the tub, I rubbed my hand over the gleaming white porcelain. It was cool to the touch and so inviting that even though it wasn't Saturday, I just couldn't resist getting into the thing and having myself a bath. For the next hour I enjoyed myself like a polar bear on a cake of ice in the summer sun, splashing about in the cooling water of the tub until water flew all over the place. Adding to the pleasure of the bath, the soap smelled just like the perfume the girls used back home and I felt pretty fancy by the time I got out of the tub.

The job of shaving was over with in a hurry, being mostly an imaginary gesture because of my youth. Now I was ready to get into my Sunday suit and step out on Broadway. The suit had been packed in my suitcase since leaving Norway and was quite wrinkled. The creases in the pants didn't show too well but otherwise it was in good shape. In fact, I cut quite a figure, I thought, looking at myself in the mirror after I got dressed in my brown speckled suit, with a stiff celluloid collar and a big yellow necktie that came almost down to my belt buckle. Nobody could tell me from an honest-to-Pete New Yorker.

With a last glance in the mirror I left the room for the lobby. I hadn't eaten since early morning aboard the ship and by this time my stomach was talking back to me. However, when I reached the lobby I found the place crowded with people milling about, seemingly going nowhere. There was nothing for the immigrant to do but wriggle his way through the chattering assemblage to the front door and some fresh air.

Out on the sidewalk I fell in with the crowd that moved like fish in a school, heading in the direction of upper Broadway while at the same time keeping an eye open for a place to eat. This drifting along with the human stream, watching the wares displayed in the shop windows along the way, was interesting enough in itself, but eventually I came to a restaurant. It had a big fish on a platter in

4

the window, no doubt to stir the appetites of fish-hungry New Yorkers. Personally I would settle for anything that would fill innards growling for attention.

I entered and found myself a small table by the window, where I could watch the crowd go by while I ate dinner. I knew ordering the food would be a problem since I couldn't read English, but there was nothing else to do but take a chance I could point at things on the menu and maybe, if I were lucky, pick the right thing.

A good-looking waitress came alongside and handed me a menu. Not wanting to let her know I couldn't read English, I just sat there for a few minutes, looking at the big card while she silently leaned on the back of my chair, chewing her gum and impatiently waiting for the order. My face got red from embarrassment, and thinking I might as well start with the beginning, I pointed to three things in a row at the top of the menu.

The waitress seemed a bit startled and said something in English that I couldn't understand. I nodded my head that it was what I wanted, so she picked up the menu and headed for the kitchen.

My first meal in America consisted of fruit cup, bean soup and clam chowder. Grinning to myself, I ate the stuff and it filled my empty stomach, but I decided that next time I would pick something farther down on the menu and maybe have better luck.

Back on the street once more, I came to a cigar store on the corner and stopped for a few minutes to inspect the wooden Indian by the entrance. Back in Norway we had seen American tourists smoking cigars, and they made quite an impression on us kids. Must be American millionaires, we thought. Stepping inside the shop I bought myself a pocketful of the biggest and blackest cigars I could find. I wanted to look like an American fast, even if it killed me. It nearly did.

That afternoon and evening were surely the most exciting in my young life. Strolling along Broadway, hat slightly on one side of my head and a big cigar in my mouth, my eyes were wide open to the wonders all about me in this strange new world filled with people rushing in every direction. There were more people than I had ever seen at one time before, even more people than we had at our National Holiday Celebration back home. It was an adventure just to walk along in the seemingly endless sidewalk parade. Nobody paid any attention to me. I was one of them now, an American!

Toward evening, my feet tired by the hard concrete, I went in to see a show on 42nd Street not far from Broadway. It turned out to be a girl show, and after a few minutes I almost wished I hadn't come in. The performers were dressed in so little, with bare legs showing away up above the knees, and they did such suggestive

5

dancing I could feel myself blushing there in the dark. Back home a show like that would have been outlawed and run out of town, but here the customers clapped and whistled for more. The legs were not bad to look at, but having been brought up a good Methodist, it made me feel guilty to be in such a place.

The show over, I went out on the street and came upon a fellow selling knockwurst from a little wagon parked by the curbstone. He looked like an Italian, swarthy, short and rather fat, with a dirty white apron across his round belly. Pausing for a moment, I said, "Knockwurst," and held up two fingers to make him understand I wanted two of them.

"Hot dogs!" he grinned back at me, handing me two of them dripping wet from the pot.

I didn't care what he called them, they were still knockwurst to me. I was starved by this time and before I had finished I ate four of them, washed down with three bottles of pop.

While I ate we carried on quite a conversation, each in his own language, much to the amusement of his other customers.

Looking me over appraisingly he said, "German, maybe?"

Between mouthfuls I shook my head, "No, Norwegian!"

"Norwegian," he mused, then pointing to the knockwurst he said, "Hot dog."

"Hot dog," I repeated, wiping the juice from my face. I walked on up the street talking to myself. "Hot dog." I had started to learn English.

It was getting late and I was dead tired. I turned into my room at the Astor just as a clock somewhere up the street struck the midnight hour. It had been an exciting day indeed, this, my first day in America.

The next morning I awoke early and lay there a long time looking up at the white ceiling of my room and pondering where I should go next. One thing was sure, I couldn't stand to live in the city permanently; it was much too big and confusing. I wouldn't know where to begin finding a job nor a place to live, and the Astor was out of the question at $2 a day. No, I must go farther into America.

Having no friends or relatives in the country, I had thought of going west to Minnesota or perhaps North Dakota. I had heard there were many Scandinavians in those states and it might be easier to get a start there in my new life. But, after one day in New York, the thought of becoming a farmer in the Dakotas just didn't appeal to me any more. I wanted to see more of the country while my money held out.

6

Lying there idly rubbing the concrete sidewalks out of my aching legs, I noticed a picture on a wall of my room. It showed a city with a waterfront and sailing ships at the docks. In the background the houses were built in neat rows along the rise of the hills. It looked almost like the pictures I had seen of the coast cities of Spain and southern France, but the inscription underneath read, "San Francisco, California, 1898."

In a moment I was on my feet, studying the picture at closer range, viewing the houses with the rolling hills behind them and the wharves where the ships were unloading their cargo.

"San Francisco," I spoke out loud. "Now that would be the place to go, almost like back home, with water and ships and things." The more I looked at the picture the better I liked what I saw. My mind was made up: I was California bound.

Happy and whistling I wandered into a dining room right off the lobby, an eating place I hadn't seen the day before. I suppose I had been too excited and walked right past it.

A friendly waiter handed me the menu and at the same time said something in English that must have been a breakfast suggestion. When I nodded my head and said, "Yes," he picked up the menu and took off for the kitchen.

Shortly he was back with eggs and sausage, and some kind of fruit on the half shell that squirted me in the eye every time I tried to dig my spoon into it. But I couldn't have ordered anything better if I had understood English. It certainly was a perfect beginning in this land of millionaires.

In the lobby I had little trouble getting information about a train to California. The clerk could not understand my Norwegian but was very helpful and patient in trying to interpret my signs and grunts. When I mentioned San Francisco he said something in English, then put his finger on the date of a desk calendar and asked, "Today?"

I nodded my head. He turned to the clock on the desk and pointed his finger at 7. We understood each other. The train would leave for San Francisco at 7 this evening.

In 24 hours in America I had learned "hot dogs," "train," "seven," "o'clock" and "room"—not bad for my first day's English. I felt very proud of my accomplishment.

Using my legs for transportation, I spent the rest of the day sightseeing. It was mostly around Broadway and 42nd streets, and forever after Times Square became New York City to me. However, now that my mind was made up for California the glamor had somehow gone out of New York, and it was only a matter of passing the time until the train left that evening.

7

About 4 o'clock in the afternoon I was down in the lobby with my bag and bundle, ready to go to the railroad station. But here I ran into another problem—how to get there. The new clerk on duty was not as patient and friendly as the one I had spoken to earlier in the day. After I paid my bill for the room, I asked the direction to the station but this fellow only shook his head and grinned at me.

After trying several others around the lobby without getting the information I needed, I picked up my luggage and went out the front door to the accompaniment of laughter. However, I too had to laugh at my predicament. I suppose I did look funny in my old-country clothes and my newcomer ways.

Out on the sidewalk, I set my bag and bundle down by the curb and dug from my pocket a brand-new map of the United States that I had bought the day before. Turning to the driver of the only auto taxi by the curb, I unfolded the map and pointed my finger at San Francisco.

For a moment the driver blinked his eyes and looked at me rather funny, then he opened the door with a flourish. He said something that ended with "Sir," as he helped me and the baggage inside.

A bit apprehensive at first about this new adventure, I sat bolt upright in the seat, watching him crank the thing and climb into the driver's seat. He adjusted his goggles and gloves, then without warning the engine sprang into action with a roaring noise and cloud of smoke. The jerk sent me flying against the back of the seat. By the time I got my hat back on my head and generally gained my composure, we were a couple of blocks down the street and going like the wind.

I didn't know how far it was to the station (I found out years later that it was only about eight blocks) and I think he must have driven me all over Manhattan. About an hour later he pulled up in front of our destination.

The bill came to $3, which was capital in those days, but I gladly paid. It had been my most exciting experience in New York.

Westward to Adventure

2

At the railroad station the giant clock on the wall told me it was 5:30. It would be another hour and a half before my train left for the West. Luck was with me, though, for the ticket agent turned out to be a second-generation Norwegian who understood me and my travel problems as an immigrant.

He had no customers at the window at the time, and was very friendly and helpful. While filling out the five-foot-long ticket, he told me among other things that I would have to change trains in Chicago and travel on a different line to San Francisco.

He also mentioned that at mealtime there would be a white-uniformed Negro waiter coming through the car, calling out dinner or whatever meal it was, and that if I wanted to eat I should get up from the seat and follow the man to the dining car.

With the ticket filled out and paid for, he said, "Maybe I better put it down on paper so you won't be confused and forget."

He wrote on a long piece of paper all the things I should do for my well-being on the journey and tucked it into the envelope with the ticket. I shall be forever grateful to that gentleman, for his kindness solved a great many of my problems on the trip.

The hour or so of waiting proved most fascinating, watching the crowd rushing through the station in a steady stream and listening to the man calling: "Train going to bla, bla bla!" His voice reverberated around the high ceiling, into a jumble of words that made me wonder if anybody could understand him at all.

At 6:45 the man called out: "Train for Chicago!" and it was my turn to jump into action. Grabbing my bag and bundle, I joined the throng going through a narrow iron gate where a man in uniform checked my ticket. Once through the gate I walked past a long line of cars before I came to the first passenger car, then I went on to board as close to the engine as I could get. This was my introduction to a locomotive, and I was intrigued.

I had, of course, seen many pictures of locomotives in the *Illustrated Weekly* in my hometown, but here I had a firsthand look at one, huffing and puffing and anxious to be on the way to Chicago. It was so absorbing that I might have been left behind if the conductor hadn't hustled me aboard and into a stuffed black leather seat in the smoking car.

9

A few moments later, to the tooting of the whistle and the clanging of the bell on top of the engine, I was off on my adventure into the wilds of America, to the stamping ground of Buffalo Bill, Texas Jack and a host of other western heroes I had read about in magazines back home.

Slowly and with much groaning and squeaking as the wheels ground the steel rails, the train wound its way out through the railroad yards and onto the open track. We traveled not west as I had anticipated, but straight north, following a great river. A quick look at the map I carried proved it to be the Hudson. At first this worried me a bit, but following the railroad lines on the map I could see where the train did head west, after we came to a town called Albany up the river 100 miles or so.

Settling back into the seat, I watched the sailing sloops and schooners intermingled with a few steamers making their way up this great waterway. I am sure no passenger on the train enjoyed the beauty of the Hudson and the hills beyond more than I did on that train ride. With my eyes glued to the window, my pulse beat in time to the clickety-clack of the wheels beating upon the rails while the strange new landscape flew by.

It had all been too exciting to think of food until a waiter in a white coat came through the car calling out something. Quickly I dug the directions my Norwegian friend had given me out of my pocket and read: "When Negro in white uniform comes by calling out meals, if hungry, follow him to the dining car."

In a moment I was on my feet making my unsteady way right behind him from car to car until we finally arrived at what must be our destination.

Tables covered with white tablecloths lined both sides of the aisle, and many happy people chatted and dined beneath the bright light from the ceiling lamps. White-uniformed waiters hurried about with trays of good-smelling food that made my nose quiver with delight for I was nearly starved by this time.

Finding myself a seat at a small table by the window, where I could see the river, I pulled the paper from my pocket again to read what I should do next. There was no advice, though, about ordering a meal.

Oh well, I thought, I'll just wait and listen to the man across the table as he orders, and I'll say the same thing.

The man didn't say a word. He just studied the menu for a moment, then wrote something on a paper pad and handed it to the waiter. Just my luck, I thought as I watched the waiter head for the kitchen with the order, to be sitting with someone who can't talk.

I was about to give up and once more point to something on the menu, taking a chance on the results, when a man sitting across the aisle pointed at something on his menu. To his woman companion he said, "Roast bee finapple pie."

I had no idea what it was, but kept repeating it over and over to myself until the waiter stopped at my table to take my order. I nonchalantly said, "Roastbee finapplepie."

The waiter must have got the idea that my English wasn't too good because he did the writing for me and hurried to the kitchen. I wondered what the culinary surprise would be, but he didn't leave me in suspense very long. He returned shortly with the most delicious food I had had in America so far, roast beef and apple pie.

After finishing dinner I lingered on in the dining car for a while, enjoying a cigar and watching the ever-changing scenery of the Hudson.

The sun was already down and the high hills across the river to the west were fast fading into the shadows of the night. In the houses along the shore lights came on, reflecting their tiny fingers

of silver in the dark waters. To me it was like a journey through a fantastic fairyland, so unlike anything I had ever seen before.

The waiter cleaning up the car for the night brought me out of my pleasant reverie and I made my reluctant way back through the swaying cars to my smoking car seat at the head of the train. Here I watched the lights go dancing by and heard the bells ringing at the station crossings until drowsiness and the comforts of a full stomach put me to sleep.

It was about noon the following day when we reached Chicago. Here I had to change to the Union Pacific Line. Noting the schedule, I found there was a layover of several hours which would give me an opportunity to explore the city. However, my explorations were confined to a very limited area, about as far from the railroad station as I could still see the big Union Pacific sign.

11

Strolling along the dirty streets, I got the impression that Chicago had more saloons than anything else. Through the swinging doors came the sound of noisy customers, a whiff of stale beer and an occasional drunk being thrown out of the joint.

I didn't know for many years afterwards that every city has its skid row, a more-or-less temporary roosting place for the down and out. Had I gone a few blocks farther, I would have come into the Loop section, the heart of a most fascinating city. But I was afraid I would get lost and miss my train.

Farther along toward the Loop the street became a bit more civilized, with stores of diverse kinds that make interesting window shopping for a stranger.

Stopping in front of a clothing store, I admired a brown suit in the window. It seemed to be just my size and I could picture myself in it, peg pants and all. It would really make me look like an American, I thought. It was hard to resist, especially when a smooth-looking clerk in the doorway beckoned me inside.

The coat fitted me perfectly. Looking at myself in the mirror admiringly, I knew there were no two ways about it, I just had to buy it. It was such an improvement over the green old-country suit I was wearing. I would have put the pants on, too, and worn the suit out of the store, but the clerk made me understand there was no place to change. So I paid the $15 and he quickly took the suit to the back of the store where he put it in a neat cardboard box that I proudly carried under my arm until train time.

Weary from pounding the concrete sidewalks, I wound my way back to the station for a cooling drink from the public water spigot and a chance to sit for a while. It was only May but the heat of the city was to me almost unbearable. Sweat ran down my face as it might on the hottest day in Norway.

The station, like the one in New York the previous evening, was filled with people coming and going in a steady stream, but here it seemed they were more relaxed and casual, with more friendliness than in the East. Perhaps it was the spirit of the West manifesting itself already.

At 6 o'clock in the evening they called the train for San Francisco. Like a seasoned traveler, I picked up my belongings and walked out through the gate where the conductor clipped off another piece of my ticket.

Again I found a seat in the smoking car up front where I could watch the engine going around the curves and hear the chugging of the monster as we moved along. I had an entire seat to myself and proceeded to make myself at home for the long trail ahead by spreading my things out on the cushion beside me.

12

Promptly at 6:15 the trainman outside my window waved his arms and called, "All aboard!" The engineer up ahead gave a couple of toots with the whistle. We were on our way West. For a while we wound our way slowly through railroad yards, and from my seat I could see factories with smoking chimneys in almost every direction.

Once in a while we passed close to them and I saw hundreds of dirty, tired men emerging through the gates from the day's labor, dangling their empty dinner pails and wiping the sweat from their faces. One thing sure, I told myself while watching them walk up the street, that kind of job was not for me. It was like being a slave and I valued my freedom and open air too much for that.

After what seemed miles of railroads and factories, we left Chicago behind and came out on the open prairie where farmers were tilling their soil in the last rays of the setting sun. Great fields of newly planted land stretched away in the distance and here and there were snug farmhouses half hidden in greening groves of trees. Herds of cows waited by red barns for milking time. Here were scenes of peace and contentment much more to my liking than the cities I had seen so far.

Yet, this was not for me either. I wanted outdoor work with action and excitement, a chance to prove my worth. Had I known then what lay ahead of me in the next few months, I might have been glad to accept one of these civilized jobs. Again, maybe not, for the spirit of adventure stirred within me and shortly I was to experience more hair-raising adventure than most people get in a lifetime.

Just before dinner, as the train rolled on, I took the box containing my new suit to the men's room to try it on, my face aglow in the mirror with anticipation. My joy was short-lived indeed. Opening the box I found not the handsome brown suit I had paid for, but an old dirty castoff suit many sizes too big for me.

For a moment I stood there stunned, burning with indignation and cursing the store clerk in my choicest Norwegian. Then I threw the filthy garment in the wastebasket. I promised myself that someday I would be back in Chicago and punch the crooked bastard in the snoot. It had taught me a valuable lesson, however, never to let anybody make a sucker out of me again.

The unpleasant incident in Chicago was soon forgotten as the train sped toward California. I thrilled to the immensity of the western prairies as they fulfilled a boy's dream to see the American frontier and become a part of it.

The locomotive was, of course, burning coal and spewing a constant stream of smoke, soot and cinders back over the train and

13

through open windows. It kept me busy digging cinders out of my eyes and wiping smudges off my face until I got wise and kept my face away from the opening. However, such little inconveniences never kept me from enjoying the journey.

The day after leaving Chicago we stopped at a hustling little town called Omaha. Girls came out from the eating house close by the station, ringing bells to announce that lunch was ready, and everybody made a rush for the place. Inside it was very warm and packed with hungry travelers. Quite a few flies had got in ahead of us, to buzz around the plates while we ate. Everybody including the girls waiting on the tables seemed to be in a hurry, so instead of trying to select something from the menu I just said, "Roast beef and apple pie," and got it.

Two elderly ladies sat at the same table I did.and kept talking to me all through the meal. Of course I didn't understand a word of the conversation but smiled back at them and we all had a good time.

After lunch everybody walked along the wooden platform in the sunshine while waiting for the train to get under way again. I was especially interested in watching a sternwheel steamer bucking the current in a big river just below the station. It was the first stern-wheeled ship I had ever seen. We never used ships like that in Norway.

A couple of toots of the train whistle brought our visit to Omaha to an end. The conductor, a short, fat, red-faced fellow, took the toothpick out of his mouth long enough to call out the familiar "Aboard!"

In a few minutes the station platform was empty except for a few native hangers-on, and we were on our way again, rolling westward through Nebraska.

In Cheyenne, Wyoming, I saw my first real cowboys, exactly as they were pictured in the books at home. When the train stopped at the station, there were people on the platform wearing big cowboy hats and boots. A few had clanking spurs and their legs were encased in leather chaps. This was indeed cattle country, something to write home about to my doubting old schoolmates.

I would have been satisfied just to sit there enjoying the platform panorama, but above the sound of hissing steam from the locomotive came loud noises and sharp whistling. A bunch of

14

cowboys were driving hundreds of cattle into corrals near the track, for shipping to market.

I craned my neck through the open window, then left the train as though shot from a cannon. I ran up the track to see them at close range. They were the real thing, sweating and whooping it up as they drove the stubborn steers into the enclosures.

I forgot all about the train until the engineer blew the whistle and the train started moving. Out of breath from running, I caught the handrail of my coach and swung aboard just as the conductor was about to close the door. He mumbled a couple a new English words for me to remember, "Damned fool."

The remainder of the afternoon passed swiftly as the train chugged over the hills to Laramie, another cattle town where it stopped long enough to take on water and coal, then rolled on into the sunset.

The landscape was changing fast now, with high mountains to the south of us that—according to the map spread out on my lap—should be in the state of Colorado. Another row of snow-clad mountains, reflecting the last rays of the sun in a pink glow, reached northward as far as the eye could see.

The plateau country showed little sign of civilization except for an occasional ranch house sitting in the wide wilderness of sagebrush and buffalo grass. We saw no people except a couple of Indians riding their ponies close to the railroad track. For a moment, in a show of hilarity, they spurred their ponies into a fast gallop trying to keep up with the train. The passengers waved them on through the windows, encouraging them to greater speed, but they were soon left behind in a cloud of dust.

It grew dark and stars came out, but the prairie disappeared from view. Being hungry again, I made my shaky walk through the length of the train to the diner, for another supper of roast beef and apple pie.

I went back to my smoking car seat and settled against the leather cushion, happy and satisfied. With feet resting on the seat ahead, hat down over eyes and a cigar butt clamped in my teeth, I slept while the train rolled on in the night.

I awoke early the next morning with the jerking of the train and the squealing of brakes. Looking out the window, I found we were winding our way down through a narrow canyon with sheer rocky cliffs on either side of the train. This scene continued until we reached the flatlands of the Great Salt Lake Desert.

Just ahead lay Salt Lake City, glistening in the early morning sunshine. This was a city to which I felt a strange kinship and knew more about than any other place in America.

15

About a year or two before I left home, a couple of young Mormon missionaries from Salt Lake City came to my hometown in northern Norway to preach their religion and gain converts for their faith. They were two likeable young men who spoke Norwegian fairly well, but they found tough sledding among the hard-core Lutherans and the handful of other denominations.

My father, being a real Christian who belonged to the Methodist brand of religion, felt sorry for the young fellows and invited them home for a square meal or two. After that first visit, the whole family liked them so well that our home was open to them forever after. We spent many interesting evenings listening to them tell about the struggles and success of those fine people in the Salt Lake Desert region.

Now that I was in their city, I couldn't resist the temptation to get in touch, at least stopping long enough to say "hello." But here I had a problem, because I had forgotten the name of one fellow altogether, and remembered only that the other one was Hendriksen.

Inquiring in the railroad station, I found there were plenty of Hendriksens in the city, so many I hardly knew where to begin looking for the right one. Then a second-generation Dane came to my rescue. He had a job in the station and could speak Danish fairly well. After I told him who I was looking for and why, he put on his hat and coat and took me up the street to some kind of office. He introduced me to another gentleman who could speak my language and who at once set about making me feel at home.

With such graciousness and such an enthusiastic reception, I forgot all about the train. In the meantime, it had gone on its way to California. This worried me until one of the men told me he would have my baggage held at the station in San Francisco and I could take a later train to my destination.

For the next three days I enjoyed the hospitality of some of the finest people I had ever met, and was treated at every turn like a prince instead of an immigrant. Christian kindness that we had shown the two missionaries in Norway came back manifold, and it reminded me of what I had read in the Good Book: "Cast your bread upon the waters, for thou shalt find it after many days." (Ecclesiastes 11:1)

On the third day, in the evening after a big dinner with my new-found friends, they took me to the train in a buggy pulled by two spirited black horses, as if I were really a dignitary of some sort. Then after much handshaking and wishes for a good journey, I bade good-by to Salt Lake City and turned my eyes to the west once more.

This would be my last night on the train. In the morning we should be in San Francisco, the end of my journey for a while. What would I do after I got there? Of that I had not the slightest idea and dismissed it from my mind as something that the future would take care of without any meddling from me.

Meditating on the three happy days among friends, I sat there looking out the open window at the shadowy outlines of distant mountains and canyons as the train chugged its way across Nevada.

San Francisco 3

It was early in the morning when we arrived in San Francisco. I had slept so soundly that I had not heard the conductor call the station, and when I awoke my fellow passengers had already filled the aisle with their baggage, ready to get off the train.

Rubbing the sleep from my eyes, I gathered my belongings together, put on my shoes and coat, and joined the crowd getting out of the smelly smoking car into the fresh salty air.

Outside the station I hardly knew where to go. Fog hung like a gray curtain over the city and I was confused as to which way was uptown to a hotel. Good luck was still with me, though. I discovered a number of horse-drawn carriages parked along the curb, some with the names of hotels painted on the sides.

One was marked "The Palace" and the uniformed driver, eager for business, took my bag and bundle and helped me into the contraption, a six-seated wagon-like carriage with a flat top overhead and fancy fringes dangling from the edges. In a few minutes every seat was taken, the driver flicked his whip over the horses' backs and we started off up the street at a frisky pace. Bouncing and swaying over the rough cobblestones, my mustachioed companions had to use one hand to hang on to the

17

seat and the other to keep their derby hats from going overboard. Never having ridden in such a rig before I thought it was great fun.

We arrived at the hotel just as the morning sun came peeking out of the fog bank, and swung in under an overhang that took us right to the lobby door. Doormen in livery were waiting to help us out of the carriage and take care of the baggage.

After only one week in America I had gained a great deal of confidence and had learned enough English to take care of myself.

It was with much pride that I addressed myself to the clerk at the desk with the well-rehearsed words: "I wish a room."

That gentleman understood me and pushed forward the registry book. I signed my name with the flourish of a well-seasoned traveler.

"Norway," he said with a pleasant smile as he noted the name and address in the book. I nodded and smiled too.

The bellboy took my baggage up to the room while I went to the restaurant near the lobby to get breakfast. I selected from the menu as usual, but this time I surely must have pointed at the right things for I had an excellent meal of hot cakes and sausages. To my surprise it was not as expensive as in New York. The entire meal came only to 30 cents. In a mood of spendthriftiness, I doubled my usual tip and left 10 cents for the waiter's fine services.

It had been a long and dusty trip across the country and I felt tired and in need of a bath. Refreshed by the bath, I stretched out on top of the bed and slept nearly the clock around.

When I finally awoke the sun had gone down and my room was dark. From my window I had a perfect view of famous Market Street, all the way from the ferry building on the waterfront to where it disappeared among the hills in the other direction. The street was distinctly outlined with a row of yellow gaslights and store windows that revealed late shoppers and strollers along the elegant avenue.

The street itself was filled with horse-drawn hansom cabs, quite a number of automobiles, and along the center section streetcars lumbered from block to block. It was not the hectic traffic of New York City, but a well-ordered movement on a street wide enough to take care of all the different types of transportation.

For a long time I stood there with my arms resting on the window sill, enjoying the view until the smell of steak and frying onions came drifting up on the evening air as a pleasant reminder that it was time to get some dinner.

The dining room in the Palace Hotel was filled with elegantly dressed people. Most of the men wore fancy dinner clothes like men wore at weddings of the rich in Norway. The ladies were dressed in

18

long gowns that reached almost to the floor. Big plumed hats, gloves and parasols completed their costumes.

The strains of a Vienna waltz played by a small orchestra made my feet glide over the floor as I followed a waiter to a table on one side of the room, where I had a perfect view of the crowd.

Must be all millionaires, I thought. I glanced down at my green old-country suit. It reminded me of a painting I had once seen, entitled *Poor Boy at the King's Court*. I was embarrassed but nobody paid any attention. They were eating and chatting among themselves.

The waiter made me feel at ease with his pleasant, friendly manner. Taking the menu handed me, I was about to order the usual roast beef and apple pie, (which by this time was becoming a bit monotonous) and was greatly relieved when the waiter made a suggestion I didn't understand except for the word "good." I nodded approval.

That first dinner at the Palace was very good indeed, the best I had eaten in my life. To this day I can't tell you what it was.

Each day San Francisco got better. The climate was pleasant and the friendly people contributed to an atmosphere of independence and freedom. I liked it.

Having been brought up in a seafaring nation, the city's waterfront intrigued me greatly. I spent a good deal of time watching the ships of many nations come and go. Occasionally I ran into Scandinavian sailors who understood my language, and in their company I sometimes took in some of the notorious joints along the Embarcadero. These casual friends also warned me about going into this section alone, especially after dark, which helped this immigrant to learn the ins and outs of the big town.

Roving the city and using every opportunity to speak to people, my English improved by leaps and bounds and I was soon able to get along fairly well in such things as ordering in the restaurants and in reading bits of news in the morning papers.

One thing, though, was beginning to worry me. I would have to get a job very soon now, because my pocketbook was getting slimmer all the time. I knew I couldn't live in such an expensive place as the Palace much longer. There was only one answer, to find work of some sort and a boardinghouse in which to live while making my first million in America. Just how to go about it was a riddle that only time could solve.

One evening while sitting in the lobby of the hotel, I had my problem solved for me in a most unique way. In fact, it was to shape my entire future and bring me more adventure and riches than I had ever dreamed of.

It was raining hard outside. Slouched in an easy chair by the side of a big plate-glass window, I watched the rainwater run in long streaks down the glass. It was too wet to go out and much too early to go to bed. The lobby was nearly empty except for a few people wearing raincoats or carrying umbrellas, hurrying in on the way to their rooms.

I was about to go to my room too, when an old man came and sat down in the chair next to mine. He must have been in his forties, but that was old age to me at that time. He impressed me as being a man of wealth and importance with his expensive-looking clothes and a watch chain made of gold nuggets across his vest.

For a few moments I watched him out of the corner of my eye, then hesitatingly struck up a conversation in my newly acquired English that he didn't seem to understand too well. But, being a good-natured fellow, he tried hard to get the meaning of what I said.

During the conversation I must have used some old-country words mixed in with my English because suddenly a big grin spread over his face. Turning toward me, he addressed me in my own language. "If you speak Norwegian, my boy, I can understand you much better."

I had to laugh. Here I had been trying to make myself understood in clumsy English to one of my own countrymen. After that we chatted mostly about the old country until late in the evening, as I told him all the news that I could think of that would be of interest to him.

We were in the coffee shop having a late snack when he finally told me something about himself and his activities in this new land. It seems that he had just returned from Nome, Alaska, where he had taken part in the first gold strike. Not only that, he had struck it rich and was going back to Norway to settle down and enjoy his wealth.

The tale so fascinated me that for the rest of the evening I sat there open-mouthed, listening to his adventures in far-away Nome. When he pulled out of his pocket a small buckskin poke filled with shiny gold nuggets, and dumped the contents in the palm of my hand, that did it.

To Alaska I must go!

It was after midnight when we parted company. Over his shoulder he said, "Good night, boy, and good luck to you."

20

From the sleepy desk clerk I got information about trains going north, and left an order to be called at 5 o'clock. Then with my head in a whirl I went to my room.

Early the next morning, while the fog still hung low over the city, I said good-by to the Palace Hotel and San Francisco. With my bag and bundle I headed for the ferry building at the foot of Market Street. From there I got a ferry across the bay to Oakland, just in time to catch the morning train for Seattle.

North For Gold 4

I felt right at home in Seattle from the moment I stepped off the train at the King Street Station and, bag in hand, headed up the avenue in search of a hotel. It was a beautiful morning, with the sun filtering through the haze and reflecting its golden image upon a thousand windowpanes across the hillside. Trudging along up the street, stiff from the long train ride, I filled my lungs with the salty air drifting up from the bay. It was a delight to be alive.

The first hotel that caught my eye was the Frye. Shaped like a flatiron, it was situated on one end of an open space that a street marker said was Pioneer Square. I swung through the open portal with my baggage, plunking it down in front of the registry desk with the nonchalance of a seasoned traveler.

My room on the third floor gave me a wide view of Elliott Bay and the waterfront with ships at anchor, ships at the docks, ships headed out over the sound for faraway ports, trailing plumes of smoke in their wake, and tugboats darting in and out with barges in tow. Along the street next to the water were railroad cars, with locomotives shunting freight to and fro from the ships. A city so young and fresh, up and doing—so different from the cities I had seen like New York and Chicago.

After a belated breakfast in the hotel coffee shop, I walked to the waterfront a couple of blocks down a street called Yesler Way. There was no time to waste—I was sure this was my gateway to a big adventure.

I had no trouble finding the Alaska dock, because even though the big gold rush was long past, it still seemed to be the center of activities along the entire waterfront. Truckers and horse-drawn wagons were hauling supplies of all descriptions into warehouses, to be loaded on the next ship going North during the short summer season.

Elbowing my way through the crowd I found a line outside the street office, waiting for attention. Most of them were checking in baggage to go on the ship to Nome, and by the looks of the crowd I knew they were mostly greenhorns like myself. Nome still had a magic name, more than a decade after the height of the original stampede to it.

It was afternoon before I got to the man inside the office, only to be told there was no more room on the ship—all space was sold. Tired from standing in line so long, and disappointed in not being able to get a ticket, I was about to leave when a fellow Norwegian by the name of Petersen, who evidently worked for the steamship line, grabbed my shoulder.

"Just a minute, fellow," he said, "I think I can get you on."

Somebody had just changed his mind about going and had turned in his ticket. Petersen took me back to the counter, where they changed the ticket to my name.

The clerk mentioned rather casually, "This is no cabin ticket, son, but it will get you aboard, and I am sure you will make out." As it turned out, it was not even steerage but who would complain? I was Alaska bound.

Petersen did me another somewhat similar favor up in Nome a year and a half later. Seems he was always around to come to my rescue in a pinch. More about that later.

The next two days that I spent in Seattle, waiting for the ship to leave, were busy ones indeed. I went from one store to another picking out things that would be suitable for the Alaska climate. The clerks at Filson & Co. were very helpful and seemed to have had the most experience in outfitting men for the North so I did most of my shopping there. Buying only what I would need, I eliminated unnecessary weight because I probably would have to carry all my belongings on my back, in a big backpack that I acquired for the purpose. Checking the list of equipment over and over until I was satisfied that nothing of importance was forgotten, I lugged my heavy baggage down to the steamship company's office and left it there until sailing time.

On the third morning after my arrival in Seattle our ship, the *Victoria*, was scheduled to sail. She was not much to look at as ships go, broad of beam and with that squat look of a well-fed duck, but she was built to withstand the pressure of pack ice, and that she could do. To me there was never a better ship for the Bering Sea trade. Her holds loaded to capacity, she also carried a deck load of lumber, barrels and an assortment of machinery that the sailors secured with chains and ropes as a prevention against it all being washed overboard in a rough sea.

The captain and the shipping agents rushed here and there on last-minute errands, while the hissing of steam from the pop-off valves proclaimed the engineer's readiness to shove off.

Finally at 10 o'clock, just as the sun broke through the low fog banks hanging over Puget Sound, we were ready to go.

The last whistle blew and the gangplank was cast off to the cheers of a crowd 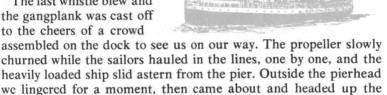 assembled on the dock to see us on our way. The propeller slowly churned while the sailors hauled in the lines, one by one, and the heavily loaded ship slid astern from the pier. Outside the pierhead we lingered for a moment, then came about and headed up the sound. From my perch on top of the deck load I watched the waving people on the dock and slowly the city faded into the haze.

With the ship under way, there was plenty of time to get acquainted with fellow passengers. Many were Scandinavians and it was nice for a change to speak and be understood. Some of the men had already been in the North and were heading back after a spree in Seattle, and from them I learned much about Nome and the gold fields.

Our accommodations were not the best but no one worried about such things. We were aboard and on our way North. Some of the rich and lucky ones had cabins, or so I was told. I never was in one of them. The poorer travelers slept in the steerage and four of us who were simply surplus slept in the hold on top of baled hay. Next to us were stacks of boxes, sacks of potatoes, flour, picks, shovels and a conglomeration of other freight useful in a mining camp. In the far corner were two horses going to Nome. Have you ever seen seasick horses?

For a week we rolled and tossed over the ocean that was anything but "Pacific." The wind coming out of the northwest sent giant waves crashing over the bow, with spray and green water flying the entire length of the ship. The good old *Victoria* took it in stride, although she wallowed in the heavy seas like a drunk going home from an all-night session at the saloon, her timbers groaning and squeaking from the strain.

23

Many of the passengers were in their bunks, fighting off seasickness and praying for an island. Others, green around the gills, made frequent, hurried trips to the rail. The only ones aboard who seemed oblivious to the wind and weather were a small group of poker players. They started the game soon after the ship left Seattle, stopping only long enough to eat and catch a little sleep before going back to the table.

One day ran into another, but I believe it was the morning of the seventh day when it calmed down a bit and we made the first landfall. Through the misty haze hanging over the sea we saw the gloomy, cold-looking mountains of Unimak Island rise over the horizon straight ahead of us. A few hours later we steamed into the inlet of Dutch Harbor.

When Russia owned Alaska, the town of Dutch Harbor was an important center for the large Russian fleet hunting seals and sea otters along the Aleutian chain of islands. Now it was only a rambling village of small houses and shacks and an old Russian Orthodox church with a typical onion-dome spire. We dropped anchor out in the bay and none of the passengers had a chance to go ashore. We would be there only long enough to unload some freight onto a barge.

While we were anchored the sun came out for the first time since we left Seattle. Everybody sat about on the deck or on top of the lumber cargo, enjoying the warmth and the view of the treeless chocolate-colored hills on shore. Those of us in the hold of the ship were especially happy to get out of our stinking quarters and into the fresh crisp air.

Dutch Harbor was busy with fishing vessels of many types, most of them dependent on sail for power. Another Alaska passenger steamer, southbound, dropped anchor a short distance from us. She was rusty and beaten, red copper showing in patches along the hull where she had been caressed by ice floes of the Bering Sea. Her decks were crowded with people milling about, trying to hear what news the captain of the *Victoria* relayed by way of a bull horn. I couldn't help but wonder, would I be southbound a year from now with my pockets full of money? Or . . . I dismissed the thought from my mind.

By midafternoon we were on our way again, heading north into the Bering Sea. In the calm of the evening we sat on the deck, watching the Aleutian Islands fade in the haze astern and the sun go down into the sea. The northern twilight lingered until about

11 o'clock, when the stars began showing in the southern sky and we descended to our quarters in the belly of the ship.

The tooting of the whistle woke us the next morning and we climbed on deck to find our ship completely shrouded in fog, so thick we could hardly see the mackinaw-clad sailor on the lookout duty in the bow. The *Victoria* barely moved through the calm water and every few minutes the whistle let out a hoarse blast.

"We are right in the lanes of the Bristol Bay fishing fleet," one of the sailors commented, "and we have to keep a close watch for them."

Of course there was no radar or similar aid to navigation, and the only way we would know the nearness of other vessels was by blowing whistles, onerous-sounding foghorns or the ringing of the ship's bells. Most of the fishing vessels were slow-moving sailing ships that had the right-of-way over the more maneuverable steamships.

About the middle of the forenoon a breeze sprang up and the fog began to lift. To the east of us, less than a quarter of a mile away, we saw a three-masted bark under full sail. She looked like a ghost ship coming out of the cloud bank, her white sails glistening like silver in the sharp light. She was sailing in the same direction and close enough so we could see the seamen in their yellow oilskins and sou'westers moving about the deck and up in the rigging. For a while we cruised along almost side by side, then slowly she fell astern and faded into the distance.

Once out of the fog belt the weather became cold and clear with a fairly smooth sea. The passengers were more restless now and even the poker game stopped for lack of interest. Instead, they moved about the ship as much as our limited deck space allowed, ever looking toward the promised land. The excitement grew when we passed what probably was Nunivak Island. Many of the men thought it was Nome until the crew informed us it would be several days before we arrived there.

On the fourth day after leaving Dutch Harbor, a low foreland came into view on the northern horizon and we knew it was Nome, the end of our journey. The sailors were scrambling all over the deck, untying chains and ropes from the cargo, and booms were being raised into position for unloading.

I had struck up an acquaintance with a young Danish fellow on the voyage and we were somewhat planning to stake a claim and work it together. The Dane was several years older than I and a smart young man, having graduated from the Danish University, but I had the advantage of being reared in the far north. I was used to roughing it, and cold weather and snow were no stranger to me.

Our languages, Danish and Norwegian, were similar so we had no trouble conversing. He seemed the kind of a fellow who would make a good partner.

Standing together on deck, we watched the land grow higher and higher on the horizon. The majority of us had never been in Alaska before and I am sure everyone was wondering what the future held in this land of gold. We were a bunch of optimists with no thought of disappointment or defeat, but only of adventure and riches in the end.

We saw the low foreland grow into a conglomeration of houses, tents, cranes and perhaps the most eye-catching, huge piles of dirt in all directions across the barren land. At first impression, Nome was a God-forsaken place indeed.

Nome 5

Because of its location, facing the open Bering Sea, Nome had no dock and we dropped anchor offshore, to wait for a barge to come and pick us up. This was not an easy task either, for the wind had increased in strength and had changed to the southwest, blowing a gale right on the beach where we would have to land.

For several hours we lay there, riding on the anchor chain and rolling like a washtub. Late in the afternoon it calmed down a bit and the captain decided to start freighting the cargo ashore.

The impatient passengers gathered at the rail with their bags, blanket rolls and diverse luggage. The more aggressive ones, elbowing their way to the front, pushed and shoved until we nearly had a fight. One obnoxious, cigar-chewing character with a derby hat pressed down over his head had a suitcase in each hand. Each was filled with bottles of whiskey that he expected to peddle to the miners. He forced his way to be first in line, much to the disgust of the rest of us.

The barge finally arrived, and after much jockeying to get in position alongside the ship, the lines were fastened after a fashion. The man with the whiskey couldn't wait. He stepped off the ship just as the barge swung away on the crest of a wave, and landed with a splash into the ice-cold Bering Sea. A sailor got hold of him with a boathook and one much-subdued peddler was hauled back aboard, to the laughter of the crowd, minus derby hat and whiskey.

The trip to shore for the rest of the passengers was rough but uneventful—except for the great relief of stepping off the barge onto solid ground once more.

On the little pier a reception committee of miners, businessmen, housewives and diverse representatives of the saloon variety were on hand to greet the newcomers. Some were looking for friends or relatives returning from Outside, others were just curious. All were anxious for news and willing to pay a good price for periodicals anyone had brought along. Nome had a newspaper, but its telegraphic bulletins from Outside only whetted its readers' appetites for fuller accounts.

I was trying to decide which way to go in this jungle of shacks, tents and material piled everywhere, when a bewhiskered fellow confronted me. He pointed excitedly at the bundle I carried and jabbered away in a language that was neither English nor Scandinavian. He was interested either in my bundle or the newspaper around it, I didn't know which. However, he took care of that. Grinning broadly through his whiskers, he peeled the newspaper off my bundle, laid the contents on the ground and handed me a $5 bill. Flabbergasted, I watched him clutch his purchase and disappear into the crowd. I wondered what he would say when he discovered that the paper was about three months old—and printed in Norwegian.

With the pack on my back, suitcase in hand and the bundle no longer wrapped in newspapers, I set off up the main thoroughfare, Front Street, in search of a place to stay. The street itself was a sea of mud and water, lined with wooden sidewalks broken off here and there and hanging in the mud. The houses looked like an architect's nightmare. They seemed to be thrown together with any kind of material at hand. They had big windows and little windows, mostly out of line and out of proportion with the one adjoining.

As I found out, the town had reached its peak a few years before and was on the decline. A recent storm had wrecked the main street, and among the buildings destroyed was one of the principal hotels. Accommodations were as short as they were during the big rush.

It was getting late and I was weary from carrying my luggage, so when I came to a two-story clapboard house with the sign, "Hotel," I went in and dropped my belongings on the floor. In the cluttered hole of a lobby I found the proprietor in the midst of a group of new arrivals, trying to convince them that the overnight price for a bed advertised on the wall at $3 was now $5. The price fluctuated with the demand each time a ship came in. He had quite a job making himself understood, for there were at least three different nationalities among the newcomers and I suspect he was roundly cursed in each language for his greed.

After much haggling about the price, everyone was taken care of and the proprietor gave his attention to me. He took me down a narrow hallway to a fairly large room filled with old-fashioned wooden army cots, each so close to the other there was barely room for a man's legs between them. When I hesitated for a moment, he assured me there were no other accommodations to be had in Nome. I reluctantly parted with five of my silver cartwheels and parked my belongings at the foot of my cot.

The room was dirty and reeked with the smell of stale tobacco and sweaty clothing. The only ventilation came from a small window high up on the wall, but after 10 days in the hold of the *Victoria* it didn't seem so bad.

Back out on the street I ran into my Danish friend, Nils. We had become separated in the excitement of getting ashore. Nils had got a bed at the Golden Gate Hotel and from what he told me, it was a much better place than the joint I was in. I promised myself I would make a change for the better on the morrow.

We decided to explore the town together, which pleased me because Nils could speak better English and there were a number of questions to be asked by both of us.

Neither of us had eaten since breakfast aboard the ship and it was now late afternoon. We entered a little clapboard shack with a sign advertising it as "Ma's Kitchen."

The place had four or five homemade tables covered with oilcloth, a few beaten-up chairs that had seen better days long before coming to Nome and a counter made out of a rough plank.

Leaning his shirt-sleeved elbows on the counter and eyeing us through steel-rimmed specs was Ma's little helper, a horse-faced gangling six-footer, badly in need of a shave. He looked more like a mucker in the diggings than a waiter in a restaurant. We were looking for food, and when he mentioned stew, we quickly agreed.

We found the stew to be excellent or maybe it was our ferocious appetites. It was mostly meat and gravy because vegetables were very expensive and hard to come by in Nome, as the waiter informed us while we ate. He pulled an extra chair up to our table and sat there pumping us for all the news he could get about things Outside. Between mouthfuls we told him all that we thought would be of interest in Seattle and points east.

Business seemed to be slow and the gentleman got into a talkative mood. He even brought over a cup of coffee for himself while telling us his experiences in the city of gold. He had come to Nome from West Virginia about a year before, with his wife who was a good cook. They thought there would be more money in starting a restaurant and feeding the miners than in shoveling gravel into a sluice box for others to get rich on. For a while they did very well, then the wife suddenly died.

"She worked herself plumb to death," he admitted, draining the last of his coffee cup.

We felt sorry for the guy, but Nils suggested we pay our bill and get out of there before he sold us the restaurant. The bill was $1.50 each, and that scared us. In Seattle one could get a better meal for 25 cents. We knew for certain we would have to get a claim of our own quickly or else a job working for someone else. Our capital would soon dwindle away with such expensive living.

At the Golden Gate Hotel I left Nils, who wanted to get to bed early. Not feeling particularly sleepy myself, I drifted along the street, watching the miners coming from the beach and the flats after a long day's work. I noticed some heading for cafes for supper, but most of them went into saloons, of which there seemed to be a goodly number.

As in most mining towns, the saloons were about the only places where men could congregate and relax after a hard day's work and the owners took full advantage of it, supplying the lonely men with the only excitement available, gambling, liquor and women.

Of course there was a better element too, the married men with their families tucked away in makeshift homes on the outskirts of town. Very little was seen of them except when they shopped at stores in the daytime. In the evening Front Street was almost entirely left to the rougher crowd.

I had just about decided to call it a day and go to bed when I noticed a long, low building across the street from the hotel. The sign over the door read, "The Northern." A number of men were going into the place and I thought it must be some kind of educational institution. Being 18 and full of curiosity, I couldn't resist the urge to find out. Crossing the muddy street, I went in too.

The Northern turned out to be the most famous, or I should say the most notorious, combination of saloon, dance hall and gambling house in Nome. The main attraction was a well-polished mahogany bar imported from Outside, with a couple of flunkies behind it dispatching drinks to the ever-thirsty customers. On one end of the bar was a pair of shiny gold scales on which the bartenders weighed the gold dust and nuggets miners paid for drinks and gambling.

In the center of the room were the poker tables, roulette wheels and other paraphernalia for separating suckers from their money. These were supervised by dealers in shirt sleeves and the inevitable green eyeshades. At the end of the room were four booths where the ladies held out. The booths were furnished with tables, old-fashioned wire-back chairs and draw curtains to insure privacy when occasion demanded.

Standing by the bar, I watched the miners coming into the place, stamping the mud off their boots and peeling off their Windbreakers, all ready for an evening of fun. Some had cash money but others made a beeline for the scales with poke in hand, anxious to exchange gold for currency. The miners were used to handling the stuff and took it for granted, but to me it was a new exciting experience to see the yellow gold trickle into the scales.

The miners were anxious to get the cash and paid little attention to the scales or the man behind them. Watching, I made an interesting discovery. The man touched his lips with his left index finger, then poured the fine gold over his wet finger into the scales. By the time the instrument balanced, he had a fine sprinkling of dust clinging to his finger, which he deftly wiped off inside his shirt pocket. No one seemed to notice what was going on or perhaps didn't care, but he probably made more money mining the miners than they did from digging in the ground.

A couple of luckless fellows who were evidently better musicians than miners, furnished the entertainment in the place. One played a guitar and the other a leaky accordian, but the music was barely heard over the whirring roulette wheels, the clicking of the poker chips and the boisterous laughter of the men.

They were not all rich, quite a number were just hangers-on who for the price of an occasional beer enjoyed the fun about as much as their luckier brethren. They were all welcome, for in this land the poor man today might be the well-heeled one tomorrow.

It was 11 o'clock and the Northern was going full swing, but having no money to spend I left to get some sleep.

At the hotel most of my roommates were snoring so loudly they could be heard out in the lobby. Once inside the room I had to wriggle over and around boots, pants and other heavy clothing scattered in every available space between the cots. This was quite tricky without waking the sleeping men, but I finally made it to my allotted space without any mishaps.

Upon inspecting my bed a little closer, I found that the mattress consisted of a thin layer of padding over a rope webbing something like a fish net. The blankets hadn't been washed since gold was discovered and were stiff from dirt and sweat, but being dog-tired from the journey, I fell into a fitful sleep.

I woke at 6 o'clock the next morning and found that all my roommates had already gone about their business. The room was empty except for me and I wasted little time in getting dressed and out of the stinking flophouse, into the fresh cold air of Nome.

At "Ma's" place I met Nils, and while we ate breakfast we discussed our plans for the day. We agreed we were absolute greenhorns in the art of mining gold and if we wanted to eat regularly we had better learn the game fast.

Immediately after breakfast we headed for the diggings we had seen on the beach when we landed the day before. The beach itself was public land that could not be staked. Anyone could work it, and did annually as storms churned up new deposits.

Moving inland, we saw men digging with picks and shovels, piling up great heaps of muck to be washed out in sluice boxes set up on stilts at an angle, with the water running through them. It was all a mystery to us at first but little by little, by watching closely each operation, we learned the process of separating the gold from the gravel.

We also saw the giant dredges that were responsible for the great ridges of dirt and gravel we had noticed from the ship while approaching Nome. These were beyond us, but wandering from place to place, we came upon a group of six men working a hole in the ground together, a hole just big enough for them to move around in. One of them manned a homemade pump that kept the water flowing over a clumsy-looking contraption they called a rocker. It consisted of several different wooden parts and a wire screen that separated the coarser gravel from the finer sand and gold, all put in motion by one of the men pulling a lever back and forth. We soon learned the basic idea and saw them actually picking good-sized nuggets off the screen. The toiling miners paid little attention to us as long as we kept out of the way and didn't ask too many silly questions.

During the day of tramping around through the diggings, we ran into a great number of Scandinavians, among them a small group of Norwegians working a claim together. When I spoke to them in Norwegian they all took time to find out where I came from in the old country. Each one wanted to know the latest news from his particular part of the Land of Midnight Sun.

One of the fellows, Ole Rapp, came from a little fishing village near my hometown. He took a special interest in us and showed us how to use the gold pan correctly, along with a hundred-and-one other things pertaining to the mining of gold. He also told us the ground around Nome had long since been staked and there was no chance of getting a claim anywhere near the town. By then, most claims were owned by companies and the men we saw working them were hired hands.

This, of course, was discouraging news but in parting he said, "Don't get discouraged, boys. Alaska is a big country and practically unexplored yet. If I were you I would get a pack together and go inland to try my luck. Who knows? You may strike a bonanza and make a million," and as an afterthought, "We would all come a-running to join you."

It didn't take much to make us enthusiastic and we decided right there that working for wages, as most men in Nome now appeared to be doing, was not for us. It was too slow for our speed. We wanted to have a fling at prospecting for ourselves. It was a million or nothing!

All the way back to town we talked and planned with the enthusiasm of youth. We would buy our equipment, get a map and head inland.

We stopped at the Northern Commercial store for the necessary supplies and gear. At best it would be a skeleton outfit because we wanted to carry enough on our backs to make do for several months. We planned to live off the land as much as possible, with meat and fish acquired along the way.

When we explained this to the storekeeper, he gave us a sad look and mumbled something about greenhorns with more guts than brains. Defensively, I mentioned that the year before, at 17, I had been a member of an Arctic expedition to Spitsbergen Island, much farther north than Alaska.

By closing time we had assembled two packs containing the bare necessities for a trip such as we planned. With a rifle and a little ammunition, each pack would be close to 100 pounds, about all we could stagger away with.

The two of us were laughing and joking about the proposed trip but the store clerk continued to have dire forebodings. He suggested that we get a job for the summer with one of the mining companies, then try our luck next season when we were more experienced. It was probably good advice and well meant, but to the impatience of youth a sheer waste of time.

We planned to leave Nome early the next morning, and spent the night in Nils' room at the Golden Gate studying our newly purchased map of Alaska. The map lacked much in detail, but we would follow a route east and slightly north, to prospect the creeks running into the Koyukuk. It all looked quite simple, traveling on the map in a nice warm room with our bellies full, but if I could have seen then the trail that lay ahead, my hair would have stood on end from fright and I would have gladly taken a humble job in Nome. Looking back on that trip, I wouldn't take a million dollars for the experience but neither would I do it again for a million.

The next morning a driving cold wind and rain swept over the area and we had to wait three days before the weather cleared. Meanwhile, we roamed the creeks learning all we could about placer operations. We returned each night to the hotel soaking wet but with increased knowledge.

I had been sleeping on the floor in Nils' room to save money. On the morning of the fourth day I awoke late, with the sun shining through the dingy windowpane.

Nils' bed was empty, and his pack and clothes were gone. On the pillow he had left a note to me, scribbled on a piece of wrapping paper: "Gone to Sunset Creek near Teller to work for a Danish friend. Wishing you luck!"

For a moment I sat staring at the paper, hardly knowing what to do next now that I had no partner. It seemed almost unbelievable that a friend should back out after all the happy anticipation and planning for the trip.

There was nothing else to do now but go it alone. The thought scared me, but after buying the supplies and food I was down to my last $10. The more I thought about it the madder I got. With a few choice words about Nils spoken out loud, I took off for the restaurant and breakfast. I would show him or anybody else that I could do it by myself.

Half an hour later, with a $2 breakfast under my belt, I headed for the hotel to get my pack. I still had $8 left, but a visit to the tobacco store took care of that. I bought eight red cloth bags of Union Leader tobacco, a strong new pipe, and in a mood to celebrate my own foolishness, a 25-cent cigar that I lit on the spot.

All the money I had left in the world was a silver quarter in my pocket. I had to make good and there was no doubt in my mind that I would.

On My Own 6

With pack on my back, Krag rifle over my shoulder and the cigar clamped between my teeth, I said good-by to Nome and was on my way into the wilderness. Nobody paid any attention to me except a Norwegian by the name of Lindeberg who had befriended me some days before. That gentleman walked along the entire length of the street trying to dissuade me from going alone. His last words on parting were: "Good luck, kid, but I know you will never come back alive!"

I guess I was about as bullheaded as they come and on many occasions paid dearly for my stubbornness, but I had faith in myself to the extreme, and sometimes in life we have to stand on that faith unwavering, without a backward look.

The city of Nome lay behind as I made my way along Norton Sound trail, passing in and out among the diggings. Men hard at work barely gave me a glance in passing, but I felt big, 10 feet tall. I was on my own!

The day passed uneventfully, just walking, walking, walking, one foot ahead of the other in a steady mechanical motion, shifting the weight of the pack occasionally by putting my fingers under the shoulder straps, first under one side and then the other. I didn't know the exact weight of the pack but I knew it was all I could possibly stagger away with. It strained every muscle in my body, clear down into the back of my legs. Sweat poured down my face and my underwear stuck to me even though the wind blew cold off Norton Sound.

About midday I feasted on one-half a loaf of dry bread that I had brought along for convenience' sake. It saved me the trouble of opening my pack, which would be quite an operation, stuffed as it was with all my worldly belongings. For dessert, my pipe filled with tobacco proved very satisfying. I leaned my back against a big boulder and enjoyed the beauty of the steel-blue waters smothered in whitecaps as far as the eye could see.

The empty pipe bowl told me it was time to go again. So on my feet with shoulder pack, and a one, two, three, four, I was on the march once more. I repeated it over and over as I marched along, speaking the words out loud to myself, and the wind carried my voice out over the emptiness of the tundra.

During the afternoon I passed several mining operations with great heaps of gravel piled everywhere. I noticed water spurting in the air from pipes used in thawing out frozen ground. It looked interesting and I stopped a while to watch the miners from a distance. They were using a monitor something like a fireman's nozzle shooting water against the frozen gravel until it thawed enough to go tumbling down into a miniature dam and through a long string of sluice boxes. There the fine black sand and gold sank to the bottom behind the riffles, and the coarse gravel and muck slushed out through the lower end of the box. But, interesting as it was, I had other and more important business of my own.

That afternoon I met two Finlanders driving a team of horses over the rutted trail toward Nome. They could speak very little English, so after a brief greeting we were on our separate ways again. They kept looking back at me for a long distance, probably wondering what such a young fellow was doing out here all alone.

The day passed until the sun was only a couple of hours high when I came to the ruins of an old stone shelter. It perhaps was built and used by Eskimo hunters some years before. It had no roof and only three walls were left standing, but it would make a shelter against the cold wind. What interested me most was that there were plenty of half-burned pieces of wood lying around, quite a find in this barren tundra.

It was mighty good to get the rifle and pack off my back, and for a few moments I had to walk around flexing the muscles in my shoulders that had become numbed. It would probably take a week or more to get used to carrying such a load.

Hungry as a bear, I set about fixing my lonely supper of fat bacon and the remainder of my bread. Perhaps by civilized standards it was not much of a meal, but the aroma of that bacon sizzling in the pan was like perfume from the table of the gods.

After supper the wind died down. I sat among the rocks for a long time, puffing contentedly on my pipe, enjoying the rugged beauty of the tundra, the blue-black shimmering waters of Norton Sound and a sky filled with more color than an artist would dare depict. The heavens were ablaze with gold, pink and many-hued reds from high overhead to the rim of the horizon where the sun was sinking.

The time must have been about 11 o'clock. I had no watch nor calendar but I wanted to keep track of each passing day by marking it down in my little notebook. On page one I wrote: "July 14th, a wonderful day!" With a last look around my camp, I rolled into my blankets and slept.

Tired from my first day on the trail, I slept late the next morning and awoke to find my little world shrouded in a wet blanket of fog that clung to the ground, limiting my visibility to a stone's throw or less. Unable to travel until the weather cleared, I just pulled the blanket up over my head and went right back to sleep in my warm nest. I don't know how long I slept, but when I awoke again most of the fog had cleared away and a feeble sun shone through the mist.

I was on my feet in a moment, shaking the dirt out of the blankets and rolling them to fit over the top of my pack. With that chore done, I built a campfire and soon had the coffee boiling and the flapjacks sizzling in the fat saved from the previous evening. I went sparingly on the coffee, using only a pinch or two for the potful. It had to last a long time and I rationed myself from the start. The aroma hanging on the chill morning air made up for the weakness of the drink.

Tobacco also must be rationed so I skipped smoking my pipe. I had made up my mind to indulge in that pleasure only after my evening meal, or perhaps if I struck pay dirt.

For the next 10 days I plodded over the monotonous tundra, one day very much like the one before. On July 25 I came to the end of Norton Sound. At that point I left the wagon trail and headed in a northeastern direction, straight for Koyukuk. I was not sure how far I had gone, but with my heavy pack, I figured my average day's travel at around 20 miles, that would put me about 200 miles from Nome.

I now had to watch my directions, constantly observing the deviation of the sun's position as the day wore on, and taking bearings on the hills ahead of me. However, I had no worries on that score for I had roamed the mountains of Norway and Spitsbergen Island and seemed to have developed a natural sense of direction that stood me in good stead now.

About midafternoon, picking my way among low hills, I ran into a small herd of caribou, about five or six feeding on the sparse grass growing among the rocks. This was indeed a pleasant discovery because my bacon supply was fast running out and I had been keeping a sharp watch for game.

The herd seemed to be working in my direction so I promptly peeled off my pack and sat down behind a big boulder to wait for the slowly moving animals to come within range of my rifle. One big problem when you backpack everything on a long trip is ammunition. The cartridges are quite heavy and you can carry only a limited amount. For that reason you have to be sure the first shot will do the job.

Sitting behind the rock, I waited until they came within about 50 yards, then picked out what looked like a two-year-old buck with plenty of fat on his carcass. Resting the rifle on a rock for better aim, I fired and the buck dropped, shot in the head. The rest of the herd scattered like leaves in the wind and in a moment were gone from sight.

That evening I celebrated with all the steak I could eat, cooked to a turn over the hot fire made from short brush that grew in a nearby draw. It was one of those pleasant evenings on the trail that lingers in one's memory. I sat there, back against a rock, puffing my pipe, watching the sun go down and the brilliant colors of sunset fade into the gray of a subarctic summer night. I was not far enough north to see the midnight sun except from some high hill, but it never became completely dark and sunrise was about 3 or 4 o'clock in the morning.

Before turning in I had to cut up the meat and select what portions to take. It would be impossible to carry all of it, so I cut out the steaks and the meaty parts of the roast. Much as I disliked it, the rest had to be left behind for wolves or foxes, who no doubt would enjoy the feast, too.

Dead tired from the day's work, I finished drinking the coffee left from supper, knocked the ashes out of my pipe and crawled into the blankets.

For the next week or two, the days passed in a routine of walking and prospecting the creeks I came to, trying my luck with the gold pan. Sometimes I worked along a creekbed for days at a time digging and panning but finding nothing that looked like gold. Perhaps I wasn't such a hot prospector yet, or maybe Lady Luck was just hiding from me. At any rate my spirits still were high and I was fast developing the true prospector's philosophy, that a rich strike lay somewhere ahead.

I was in good caribou country and my meat supply was always well ahead of starvation. I also tried my luck in the creeks with the fishhooks I had brought along. At first this was quite a task, but after a while I learned the technique and snagged many a fish dinner in the shallow waters. They were a welcome change from a diet of meat. Being raised on fish, so to speak, I could get along very well without any vegetables at all, except that a potato would have made my dinners a bit more complete.

As far as geographical position was concerned, I was nowhere near as far north as my hometown in Norway, well above the Arctic Circle with the midnight sun for more than two and a half months every summer. It is in the same latitude as Point Barrow, the northernmost point in Alaska. So, I felt at home in my surroundings, except for the mosquitoes. The first couple of weeks out I seldom saw one and on warm days dug with my bare upper body exposed to the sun. Then all of a sudden they came out of nowhere, first a few, then swarms of them arrived, covering my neck and arms.

The little stinging devils kept me in constant misery, scratching and clawing at them. But I guess every paradise has its drawbacks. I learned to keep my shirt on, and fashioned a piece of cloth into little strings that dangled from my hat, trying to scare them away while I worked. At night I slept with the end of the blanket pulled over my head, which gave me some relief from the tormentors that lay in wait for me to come back out again.

One morning in the early part of August I thought surely I had struck pay dirt. Working the gravel beside the creek, I took a few test pans as usual. Washing out the gravel, I found fine black sand and what looked like specks of gold dragging along the rim. They were so tiny it was impossible to pick them up with my fingers, yet they clung to the bottom, barely moving with the gentle slushing of the water in the pan, just as the miners back in Nome had shown me. It must be gold.

I forgot all about the mosquitoes that swarmed around my head while I dug deeper into the gravel bank, testing pan after pan beside the creek while visions of big nuggets danced in my head and spurred me on to greater efforts.

I learned the real meaning of gold fever. I could hardly take time off to eat or sleep, now that I had seen pinpoints of the yellow stuff right in my own pan. My brain was awhirl with anticipation of a big strike. My body trembled from exertion with pick and shovel. It was hard work, and to make it worse the dirt became frozen as the hole got deeper. Now I had to pick it loose and shovel it up to thaw in the sun before I could use the pan to find out if any gold was in it.

I probably would have worked all day without stopping to eat, but a black bear catching fish a little way up the stream reminded me it was time to get some food too. Leaning on the shovel handle, I watched the four-legged fisherman catch his fill of wriggling brown trout with the greatest of ease. I only wished I could do as well, but time was too precious to get into a contest with Blackie. Instead I contented myself with a chunk of caribou meat fried in the pan, and the coffee remaining in the pot since morning.

While eating, I studied a dozen or so yellow specks that I salvaged from the gold pan and that now reposed on a clean page of my notebook. Turning them over and over with the point of my knife, I became more certain that it was gold all right, and where there is fine stuff there must be coarser gold farther down, I reasoned with myself.

The black bear in the meantime had finished his fish dinner and now stood on his haunches about 100 feet away, eyeing me curiously, water dripping from his wet fur like golden droplets in the sunshine. Sniffing the air and grunting to himself, he gave no sign of being afraid, although he probably had never seen a human being before. He just couldn't quite make up his mind whether to run or to investigate me further. For a few minutes we ogled each other, then deciding I wasn't worth bothering with, he let out a low belly growl and ambled off up the creek without a backward glance.

Now that the bear was gone, I went back to digging and testing the ground with the gold pan to see if the amount of color had increased in quantity and size. Each pan that I washed showed that same few fine specks of yellow dust and nothing more. It was frustrating indeed, with so much backbreaking toil going into it. The yellow specks goaded me on like a bag of candy waved in front of a child.

Toward evening a fresh breeze sprang up out of the north. It gave me a respite from the mosquitoes and the prospect of a good night's sleep without the usual plague of little winged devils. Taking advantage of the situation, I thought this would be an ideal time for the bath postponed ever since leaving Nome many weeks before.

Right after supper, standing beside the creek, I stripped off my heavy wool shirt and pants, the only clothes I wore in the summertime to save my underwear for colder weather later on. My big yellow bar of lye soap had to be used very sparingly to last me for the trip. Rubbing a bit of soap on the dirtiest spots on the shirt and pants, I washed them out with my hands and placed the two garments in a shallow area in the water, anchoring them with a rock to prevent them from going downstream with the current. I thought by morning the motion of the water would do a pretty good job of cleaning them, and it did.

Now I was ready for my long awaited ablution. Rubbing a bit of the soap on my bare chest, I jumped into a hole in the creek about belly deep. If there had been anybody within a mile, they surely would have heard me yell. When I hit that icy cold water, it stabbed like a knife. For a few moments I jumped around like a wild man, whooping and scrubbing for all I was worth while the creek water flew and goose pimples blossomed all over my body.

With the bath over, I ran back and forth on the rough gravel, slapping my arms together to set the blood circulating again before I dressed in a fresh outfit of shirt and pants. Then I washed the dirty socks and lay them over a rock to dry.

Moments later, lying on my blankets, smoking my evening pipe and watching the sunset, I felt quite pleased with myself. Just since supper I had done a whole month's laundry.

Each day that followed for an entire week, I had nothing of any great importance to put down in my diary. My time was filled with digging deeper into the frozen gravel until I had reached a depth of about 12 feet. I still had the same few colors in the pan every time I tested the gravel, no more, no less. Frustrated and weary, I decided to move on eastward the next morning, looking for shallower ground and better luck.

Later with many years of prospecting experience behind me, I could see the situation I had faced. It was an old creekbed with perhaps 20 or 30 feet overlay to bedrock, and it would have taken more than pick and shovel to reach the bottom and the gold strata. Perhaps in later years some hydraulic outfit worked this place, or more likely, it is still lying there untouched and waiting for some lucky fellow with the right kind of equipment to come along and make a fortune.

Trapped

7

Continuing my journey eastward over hills and valleys, I stopped only long enough to dig a few holes in likely spots for a sample of the gravel, then went on my way again.

I noticed a change in the weather from the pleasant sunshine of summer to much rain and cold, a sure sign that fall was not far away. Especially on dry mornings the ground would be white with rimefrost that lasted till midmorning. Then, too, the change from all daylight, until now when the sun set about 5 or 6 o'clock in the evening, had sneaked up on me.

I had passed the point of no return. There was no going back to Nome before winter.

I knew it, yet each time the thought previously had entered my mind I quickly dismissed it. I had to make good, I just had to! The consequences of failure to do it before summer was over was something to cope with when the time came.

On the morning of September 15 I crossed a barren stretch of tundra, bearing straight east toward what I thought would be the Koyukuk River. The weather was clear except for a strange white haze hanging over the landscape to the north, and quite chilly. I imagined I could smell snow in the air, something I was well used to in my native land.

It was more than two months now since I had left Nome, but the time had slipped away so fast in my daily routine of walking and prospecting, the thought of snow and approaching winter startled me. I hadn't given much thought as to where I would spend the winter, my only resolution being that I would never return to Nome broke.

Now, I could not make it back before winter set in, even if I wanted to. I had to think and act fast if I wanted to survive.

From a rise in the tundra I could see ahead, three or four miles away, a forest stretching along the horizon to the east. This was the first real forest I had seen since leaving Seattle, and at that distance it looked exceedingly good.

Trudging along with a pack made heavy by meat from my latest kill, I had covered about half the distance to the timber when things began to happen. The white haze I had observed earlier turned out to be the first snowstorm of the season, sweeping out of

41

the north in a curtain of white, with the fury of a midwinter blizzard. The wind was so strong it nearly swept me off my feet. I staggered along gasping for breath, with my eyes fixed upon the forest that was now fast disappearing into a world of driven snow.

It seemed like hours before I finally dragged myself into the shelter of the trees and dropped my burden upon the ground. For a few moments I stood there with my heart pounding from exhaustion. Leaning on my rifle barrel, I looked back at footprints that were fast being covered by snow.

I was alone—and this time afraid!

Surveying my surroundings, I found the trees small and scrubby. The larger ones measured about six or seven inches in diameter on the big end. However, they would be big enough for a shelter, or preferably a cabin. The thought of a log cabin struck me as funny, since I had never attempted to build one. But now that I was faced with that kind of construction, it seemed no problem at all. It had to be done, which was all there was to it.

I would find a much better cabin site farther into the forest, where the wind coming off the tundra wouldn't reach me. After resting a while, I shouldered my pack and set off.

About four or five miles from where I entered the forest, I came to an ideal place to build my winter home. It was a narrow draw-like canyon with a creek running through it, a pocket snug from the wind and weather, with timber-clad hills on three sides. Here the snow came down in big quiet flakes, settling on the trees and turning the landscape into a fairyland.

My noonday meal was forgotten. All through the afternoon I worked like a beaver, building a temporary lean-to to shelter me while working on the cabin. It was a bigger job than I had anticipated, cutting and fitting the little spruce poles and boughs together so that they would shed water from melting snow. By the time I had the thing finished and had put my belongings inside, it was getting dark.

I hadn't eaten since morning, so I set about gathering dry spruce boughs. There was a plentiful supply of birch trees, too, and their bark made excellent fire starters. It took only minutes to get a roaring campfire going. The ghostly glare of fire glistening on the surrounding trees was conducive to an eerie feeling of loneliness and despair, but I caught myself up short. Such thoughts could have no place at this stage of the game.

I was young, strong, master of my surroundings and afraid of nothing, I told myself. To prove the strength of my heart to my faltering mind, I whistled a tune while frying my steaks over the fire.

It quit snowing and cleared up, and now the blazing stars danced in velvet sky high overhead. Trees with a sprinkling of snow on their green boughs stood in silent applause to the heavenly show. In the midst of it all, I, a mere man, appeared an intruder. Still, I sensed a nearness to the Great Creator. It gave me strength and peace. I was privileged, indeed, to be a part of it all.

After a supper of two large steaks that would have cost me at least $6 in Nome, I cleaned the gravy out of the pan with a piece of fat meat and ate that too. Then with my pipe going, I sat down on a log to rest.

The importance of speed was upon me, though, and I couldn't take time to relax with so much work to be done. Clamping the pipe between my teeth, I got to my feet and set about laying out the site for the cabin. I measured off a space about 10 feet by 16 feet and marked each corner with a wooden stake. Working by the light of my campfire, I cut down the brush, then with pick and shovel leveled off the ground inside the stakes. That space would be the floor of my new home. The job done, weariness from the long day took its toll, and sleepily I piled enough logs on the fire to keep it going through the night. With a last look at the stars above, I hit the sack in the lean-to.

When I awoke the next morning, the sun was already up and its sharp glare upon the new snow made me squint while getting the fire going and breakfast started. The weather couldn't have been better for the big job ahead, just cool enough for comfort, with the clean Alaska air that made it a pleasure just to be alive.

Checking on the timber, I found there were plenty of good logs to be had nearby without cutting down many near the campsite. They should be left for a good windbreak. I prepared a slim pole to be used as a measuring stick for the long poles to be placed lengthwise in the cabin wall, then a shorter one, about 10 or 11 feet long for the end walls.

Back in Norway some years before, I had seen a log cabin under construction and had watched the men notch the ends of each log to fit snugly into the next one. That recollection helped me now.

Picking four trees the right length and as straight as could be found, I chopped them down. I slabbed off the opposite two sides of each log so they would be close to one another and as weatherproof as possible. It sounds easy, but each tree had plenty of limbs to be trimmed off before slabbing the sides and that entailed much work with the ax. It had to be done, though, before they were ready to be notched and laid into place.

During the building of the cabin I missed not having a saw for cutting the logs and squaring the ends. But as I said before, one

can carry only so much weight and because of
this limitation my entire outfit of tools consisted
of one very fine ax, made from the best grade
of steel I could buy in Nome and kept
almost sharp enough to
shave with; one eight-
inch broad-
blade hunting
knife

that I
was very proud
of; and a file with
two cutting sides, coarse
and fine. Then I had another tool quite by accident, a 10-inch rusty
spike that I picked up in the ruins of the old cabin where I camped
one of the very first nights out of Nome. I had thought it just a
worthless piece of junk, but I stuck it in my pack anyway. Now it
proved to be a very valuable tool, taking the place of a drill for
making holes in logs for wooden pegs. This I did by heating the
spike red hot over the fire and burning holes wherever needed. It
proved to be just the thing for such operations.

I would never recommend going into the wilderness with such a
limited supply of tools to anyone else, but I found that with a little
imagination and a lot of patience, you can accomplish almost
anything you set out to do.

Log by log construction of the cabin progressed. By noon, or
rather by the time I got hungry (I had no watch), one complete
tier of logs was in place and several other trees were felled, ready to
work on.

I sat on a log to eat my lunch of cold meat left over from the night
before. While admiring my handiwork of the morning, I heard a
strange noise from the thicket nearby. At first I saw nothing, but
the noise of breaking limbs came again, and out of the brush a
good-sized brown bear advanced toward the clearing where I sat.
Evidently he was just as surprised as I was, because he stopped
short and stood up on his hind legs, swinging his head from side to
side, sniffing the air with an inquisitive look about this two-legged
creature that had invaded his domain.

For a few moments we surveyed one another, then I grabbed the rifle and fired. One shot brought him down. I rushed with my hunting knife to cut his throat, barely avoiding a swipe of his mighty paw in the death struggle. It was a case of hitting him with one shot and using the knife, to spare ammunition.

I had killed several bears in the old country so I wasn't afraid, yet this one had taken me by surprise. When it was all over I sat for a while on a log, trembling from nervous reaction.

It took the rest of the afternoon to skin the bear and cut up the meat, which was of prime quality. It was probably a four-year-old and rolling in fat. When I got through, meat quarters were hanging from a limb behind what would be my future cabin. My food needs were taken care of for some time to come. The skin, rather large with long glossy fur, would make an excellent fur for my floor. I hung it on a pole between two trees, intending to scrape and clean it when there was more time for such things.

With the bear taken care of, I had quite a job cleaning myself up. It took half an hour on my knees, beside the creek, to get the grease off my fingers so they would not stick together.

It was too late to go back to work on the cabin. The short subarctic day had come to an end and darkness slipped down over my little camp.

During the building of my cabin one day was pretty much like the day before. I cut down trees, slashed the sides, notched the ends and fitted each one into place. A number of times I found myself sitting on a log, scratching my head trying to figure out some of the many problems that came up. Eventually, by trial and error and after many days of hard labor, I had the walls and roof poles in place and began the tedious task of cutting shakes. This job took about as much time as the entire rest of the cabin because I could never hit twice in the same place with the ax, which gave me an assortment of shakes, some fat, some lean. Each shake had to be tight and correctly fitted to keep out water from rain or melting snow.

I had no nails so I simply tucked one end of the shake under the one above, hoping it would stay in place. That night a strong wind came up. The next morning had me on my hands and knees, picking up shakes that had been scattered all around the cabin.

This situation had me stumped for a while, until I hit on a solution. There were plenty of small flat stones lying around the creek, and one about the size of my hand on top of each shake did the trick. Then shortly after the cabin was finished, the roof became loaded with snow that stayed on until spring, so there was no more trouble all winter.

The chimney proved to be another study in wilderness architecture that took a little ingenuity to conquer. I left a four-foot opening in the end wall, facing back toward the hills, and here I constructed a fireplace and chimney out of stones, half inside and half outside the cabin, using a mixture of mud and moss to fill the cracks. It took me a week to do the job. When finished, I started a fire to see how it would draw. For a few moments it looked as if the entire cabin were on fire, smoke pouring out of holes and cracks all the way up to the top of the chimney.

Even the best of builders have their problems and I was not discouraged. I just kept pushing mud into every hole where smoke came out, until at long last it was tight and drew perfectly. I was so happy to have fire going in the cabin that I was almost tempted to move into it that evening, but the day's work had tired me too much. I just curled up in my lean-to and went to sleep there for the last time.

The final job was the door. That I made from small spruce poles fastened together with wooden pegs. The hinges I made from pieces of bear skin, and then fashioned a wooden doorlatch.

Now that my home was finished, I felt quite proud of my accomplishments. Humming to myself, I dragged my belongings from the lean-to into the cabin. There were many odds and ends to be done yet, such as making pieces of furniture. A bed, a table and a chair would certainly make living more comfortable, but such things could be done later when the weather would keep me indoors. For the present I covered the dirt floor with spruce boughs and unrolled my blankets on top. That was a big improvement over sleeping outside.

Lucky for me, the weather had stayed perfect throughout the construction period, barely enough snow to cover the ground and just cold enough for comfort. The creek remained open, too, with only a little ice freezing along the edges and melting away in the daytime when the sun came out.

Plenty of trout were swimming around in the water, and now that I had a little time to give to it, I tried my luck as a fisherman. Rigging up a fishing pole with string and a hook baited with bear meat, I sat on the edge of the creek to have some fun, but try as I would with fat meat and lean, the fish only came close to the hook, then scooted off again.

After an hour or so I was almost ready to give up. Then in exasperation, instead of meat I tied a small piece of red flannel from my shirt onto the hook. That did the trick. The trout couldn't resist. Every time the hook hit the water I had another fish, until by late afternoon I counted 34 wriggling on the gravel bank.

It took until after dark to clean the fish and hang them on long poles between the trees back of the cabin—just in case animals came snooping about. I knew there were plenty of foxes in the neighborhood, having observed them or their tracks in the snow.

With the day's work done outside, I turned my attention to a happy evening in my new home, an evening that forever lingers in my memory. The cozy warmth of the fireplace, the shadows from the fire dancing upon the ceiling and walls and the pleasant odors of trout frying in the pan, made me feel like a king in his castle.

In the spirit of celebration, I made a few pancakes to go with the fish. Pancakes were a delicacy I hadn't tasted for more than a month. I had lived entirely on meat or an occasional fish and a few blueberries picked along the way.

Before turning in for the night I sat for a long time on a chunk of wood in front of the fire, basking in the pleasant glow and puffing on my pipe. Struggle and tension had given away to peace and contentment. My mind drifted back over the past three months since leaving Nome. So many things had happened.

Adventures that I never dared dream of had become realities, and now they gave me strength of body and mind such as I had never known before. Sitting there on the log, watching the smoke spirals curl up the flue, I felt like one apart from the rest of the world, not afraid of things to come nor fretting over the fact that Lady Luck had passed me by so far. Winter just meant living through storms and snow until another summer, with faith and hope of the big strike then.

Filling my pipe again, I thought about Nome, how the boys would be whooping it up in the saloons along Front Street. And Nils, would he be there among them, spending his summer's earnings? Maybe he wondered what had become of me, too. Would we ever meet again? My mind rambled on, reminiscing of friends and places until the lonely howl of a wolf interrupted my pleasant reverie. With pipe in hand, I listened for a few minutes. I was tense because the wolves had never come close to me before, but there was no more sound from the forest, only the silence of the night and the soft crackling of the birch logs on the fire.

It was getting late and I had a big job ahead of me tomorrow, cutting firewood enough to keep my cabin warm and comfortable through the long winter months. There would be good days when I would enjoy swinging the ax to add to my supply, but knowing winter in the Far North, I also knew there would be weeks of stormy weather when it would be impossible to do any work outside. At such times my fireplace would burn a cord or two in a hurry, and my pile would disappear fast.

Touching up the edge of the ax with the file, I set it in the corner ready for the morning, took a last look out the door at the stars, and satisfied that all was well, crawled into my sleeping bag.

I was up and about long before daylight the next morning, cutting down the driest birch and spruce that would make good firewood. I dragged them near the cabin where I could cut each log into lengths to fit the fireplace, and piled them in neat rows against the side of the cabin. The birch bark I gathered to start fires.

The sweat ran down my back while I swung the ax into the soft wood. My pile grew until it nearly reached the edge of the roof, and I was ready to call it a day.

The days were getting so short now that the sun set in the middle of the afternoon, leaving behind a hazy twilight that lingered for another hour or two before it got completely dark.

With my day's work done, I stood for a while wiping the sweat from my face and watching the sun sink below the forest to the west. There was a peculiar display of color in that sunset, first the usual fiery red and gold I had observed most evenings, then strange fingers of eerie whitish clouds came stealing in from the north, moving across the face of the sun like streamers of gauze until the sun was swallowed up in a hazy gray.

With an uneasy feeling I couldn't explain, I entered my cabin, put the ax away in the corner by the door and built the fire for my supper. While it was cooking I turned to my daily calendar, the little notebook in which I put a mark for each passing day. Sometimes I missed, though, so I didn't know offhand what date it was. Counting the marks back to my last dateline, September 15, I figured it was now October 21 and a Saturday.

Being a creature of civilized habits, the thought of Saturday night gave me a feeling of relaxation from my week's work. It also suggested—of course—a bath. I hadn't had one for quite some time now, and my underwear was beginning to feel as though it were plastered on.

My bear meat dinner over, I set about the bath chore. I carried water from the creek in the only vessels I had, the gold pan and the cook pot. Stumbling over rocks and chunks of wood in the darkness, I made it safely back to the cabin where I placed the vessels over the flame in the fireplace.

By the time I had enjoyed a pipeful of tobacco, the water was warm. Placing the gold pan on the dirt floor as close to the fire as possible, I stripped off socks and shirt, then the heavy underwear. Shivering in my birthday suit, I rubbed myself with my only piece of soap. At first it didn't seem to have much effect, but after a great deal of scrubbing the real skin began to show through.

The bath over, I dug through my pack for the clean suit of underwear and made a discovery. Wrapped in the union suit was a small thermometer that Nils had given me in Nome. At that time I wanted to throw it away, but now it would provide an interesting chore, checking the daily temperature through the winter months. I put it on the mantlepiece over the fireplace, where it registered 62 degrees, a very pleasant heat for the cabin.

The following morning I fastened it permanently on the outside of the cabin wall, close to the door, and it promptly went down to 17 degrees above zero.

Little details such as these are of no consequence unless you live alone, absolutely isolated from the rest of the world, then each little thing has an important meaning.

The cabin would be my home until spring set me free to roam again. In the meantime I had to keep up with my meat supply and woodpile, and perhaps most important, be on constant guard against sickness, broken bones or other injuries. It was a case of "stay alert to stay alive!"

Winter   8

Imprisoned by winter, I scraped the fat off the bearskin, which made a perfect rug and covered most of the floor. With the fur side up it gave a coziness to the place and also kept the chill off the dirt floor.

Then I turned my attention to some other necessities. I needed a bed to get me off the cold floor, a table to eat and write on and a comfortable chair in which to spend my leisure hours in front of the fire. Not having had experience in making furniture, and with only crude tools, this would present a challenge to ingenuity.

It was too cold to waste much time in the open, so it didn't take me long to knock down the necessary timber for my projects and drag it inside. In short order my cabin took on the look of a carpenter shop and chips flew as I measured and cut pieces to make the bed. Finally with a covering of soft fir boughs and the blanket on top, it was ready for occupancy. It wasn't much to look at, perhaps, but it would keep me off the floor.

The first storms drove snow through cracks in the log walls that I had failed to chink. Now the cracks were filled with snow forced into each little opening by the wind. My cabin was completely sealed and much warmer.

After I completed the bed, I made a table from poles fastened together with wooden pegs, the tops smoothed down with the ax until it was nearly level. In front of the fireplace I placed my masterpiece, a chair made from a block of wood, with armrests and a back to lean against.

My housekeeping was quite simple. Having no dishes other than a tin plate and a tin cup, I often ate right out of the frying pan. Then instead of washing it, I just opened the door and banged the pan against the wall. The dishes were done.

The creek froze over solid and was covered with a couple of feet of snow. It didn't worry me because I could use snow in my cook pot, and it would be months before I could take another bath so there was no problem on that score. Wood cutting, of course, was my main occupation, to keep the fire going night and day.

The days and weeks slipped by in my daily routine of keeping alive. Each evening I faithfully made another mark in my notebook. Once in a while I added the marks up to determine the exact date. That became a game in itself—keeping up with the days.

The weather I had come to accept as good, bad or worse, the latter being the usual order of the day. Snowstorms came and went, each time dumping a foot or two of fresh snow, which drifted against the weather side of the cabin until I could walk right up on the roof. It had become quite cold, too. Some mornings the thermometer registered 30 or 40 degrees below zero, but the air was so dry and still it didn't seem nearly as cold as that. After getting my nose frostbitten a couple of times, I paid more attention to the scientific contraption hanging on the cabin wall and covered up a bit more when working outside.

The inside of the cabin was quite comfortable even on the coldest days. The front half near the door was covered with white hoarfrost that grew like whiskers under the roof beams and walls, but the half near the fireplace took on a glazed look from soot and heat from the fire. The edge of my blankets nearest the wall froze to the logs and stayed that way most of the winter, but I slept warm.

One evening I took the thermometer inside the cabin just to see what it would register. Hanging it on the wall a little distance from the fireplace, I waited an hour or so then checked the temperature.

It was 56 degrees. Next I hung it inside the door on a hoarfrost-covered log. After a while it registered 24 degrees. You can see why I confined most of my activities to the warmer end of the cabin.

One frosty morning I stuck my head outside the door to fill my pot with some snow for the morning coffee. Several caribou were feeding on the bark of the young trees, as calmly as if they were barnyard cattle. My meat supply was getting dangerously low, so I shot three of them, each with one bullet. Now I had all the meat that I could use for the rest of the winter.

The three caribou skins made a good addition to the bear rug already on the floor and gave the cabin an air of warmth and snugness. I could even walk around in my stocking feet on the hairy surface and enjoy it.

Cabin Fever 9

One evening, counting the black marks in my notebook, I discovered the date was December 23. Christmas was only two days away. In Norway Christmas is a three-day affair, the biggest event of the year. Everyone drops all thought of work to eat, drink and be merry. I wanted to make it a real old-country Christmas such as I used to have at home, a thought that made me laugh at myself. Here I was, hundreds of miles from nowhere and yet the Christmas spirit filled me with excitement.

Following up the thought with action, I pulled on my sweater and rushed out in search of a suitable Christmas tree. The moon was high overhead, lighting my way as I walked in and out among the spruce trees, singing at the top of my voice the old familiar *Silent Night*.

There was a plentiful supply of trees to choose from, but like a shopper back in the States, I was particular and had to find just the right tree. Wandering from one to another and shaking the snow off for a better look, I settled on a neat little spruce about three feet high. A couple of whacks with the ax and I hurried into the cabin with my prize.

I worked far into the night, building a foot for the tree to stand up on the table. The decorations were a problem, but when it was finished I was proud of my creation.

The limbs were decorated with the tin foil from my tobacco bags. The red cloth from the outside of the bags I cut into thin strips and strung them around the tree from limb to limb. The masterpieces of the evening were the candles that I made from frozen bear grease, shaping each one by rolling a lump on the table until the grease melted just enough to round up. A short piece of yarn from my heavy wool socks, pushed into the center with the point of a knife, furnished the wicks. By heating the small end of my file red hot, then using it to burn little holes in the tree limbs, I inserted a small wooden peg. The other end of the sharp peg went into the candle.

On Christmas Eve, with a roaring fire in the fireplace, the candles aglow with tiny yellow flames, I sat in my chair toasting my toes in solitary peace with the world, a juicy hunk of bear meat in one hand and a piece of bannock in the other. Bannock is prospector's bread made from flour and water and I had been saving my last dab of flour for this occasion.

After the big dinner I went outside on the snow. The moon, high overhead, was a full silver disk on a background of dark blue. Off to the northwest the northern lights waved softly in many-colored hues of pink, yellow and green. The trees loaded with snow made short stubby shadows. A brooding silence hung over the land.

The thermometer on the cabin wall registered 62 degrees below zero. Shaking from the cold, I began singing Christmas songs in

Norwegian at the top of my voice. In a moment the wolves joined me from somewhere in the brush with long melancholy howls. Maybe they couldn't take my musical outbursts. My nose began to feel numb from frost, so with a last *Gladelig Jul*, I ducked into the cabin and pulled the door shut behind me.

My thoughts took flight across the expanse of snow and ocean to Norway and home, where they were celebrating Christmas, too. The family hadn't heard from me for months, and deep in my conscience there was a feeling of guilt. I should have written from Nome. I deserved a good kick in the pants and would gladly have bent over for the operation.

By now my supply of coffee was so slim I had been boiling each pot over and over, sometimes for a week at a time, until the concoction became so thin it had little coffee taste left. In January and February the loneliness began to get the best of me. Storm after storm swept over my little valley and I became a prisoner of the weather, spending most of the time walking the floor or just sitting by the fireplace. At first there was work to be done repairing my clothes and boots, but after a while this gave out, and the wear and tear on my nerves began to show.

As the days dragged on, I suffered from sleeplessness, sometimes waking up in the middle of the night soaking wet from sweat and trembling like a leaf from fright of being alone. But I found an excellent remedy for that, and wondered afterwards why I hadn't thought of it sooner. When I seemingly had reached the end of my rope, I would jump out of bed, open my little Bible with trembling hands, and by the light of the fire read out loud for 15 or 20 minutes. Like a dying man receiving a blood transfusion, my mind and body responded and strengthened with each verse until my spirits rose from despair and my fears took flight into the night. I knew that I was not alone. After such a session I usually wound up in a happier mood, singing the old familiar hymns in Norwegian that I had learned at home.

In the latter part of February the sun was visible for three or four hours in the middle of the day, and after sunset the twilight lingered on until quite late in the afternoon, giving me much more time to work outside cutting wood and exploring the countryside around my home. I was anxious to find out if there were any signs of human beings other than myself, perhaps other cabins in the vicinity.

The country to the northeast I found to be very rugged with one narrow canyon-like valley after another, covered with scrub timber of the same variety that grew around my cabin. The trees were mostly young spruce, a scattering of white birch and a variety that I didn't recognize, but took to be either aspen or elder. These good-weather journeys took me farther and farther from home each time, until I knew the country pretty well within a radius of four or five miles.

Many times when the weather was clear, I stopped cutting wood to admire the beauty of a large hill, or rather a small mountain, which seemed to be about 15 or 20 miles away to the northeast. In my diary I called it "Old Baldy" because the bottom half was covered with timber and snow covered the top half. It stood out pink and purple in the last gleam of the setting sun. I promised myself that as soon as the weather permitted, I would climb the lofty heights for a better view of the surrounding country.

But first I had an important job, making myself a pair of durable moccasins that would keep my feet warm and save wear and tear on my only pair of boots, which had really taken a beating while walking over the rugged rock-strewn country. I wanted to save what was left of them for the journey back to Nome.

It was my first experience in the art of being a cobbler. Selecting the heaviest caribou skins in my collection, I began the job by stretching the skin on the cabin floor and scraping it perfectly clean of fat and grease. This I did with the sharp edge of a flat piece of stone, until the skin appeared to be dry and fairly pliable. After that operation, I went over the entire skin again, pounding it with a round stone to bring out the hidden oil or fat until it again seemed quite greasy. Another scraping with the stone got rid of the residue and it was ready for marking and cutting.

Leaving the skins with the hairy sides down, I placed my stockinged foot on top of the smooth side and drew the outline with the point of my hunting knife. Then I drew another line about 10 inches farther out on the skin so it would fold up over my foot and form a top above my ankle. It was a slow and tedious job, but after many trials and errors the cutouts were ready for the job of sewing them together.

Back in Nome someone had suggested that I take with me a shoemaker's awl, and I shall be forever thankful for the suggestion. The awl was a most useful tool in sewing the skins together, using prewaxed sail yarn for the job.

It took me three days to complete the job but when finished I was very proud of my accomplishment. Each moccasin was a two-layer affair with one hairy layer outside on the bottom, and the other hairy side on the inside to keep my feet warm.

The morning of February 27 seemed to be a perfect time for undertaking the journey to Baldy. The snow was packed solid with a harrd surface for walking, the wind very normal and the thermometer stood at two above zero, an excellent combination for the long hike.

Taking the rucksack from the peg on the wall, I put into it enough food to do me for a week or more. I also put in a few spare cartridges for the rifle, matches and odds and ends that would be needed should a storm come up.

Daylight that came about 9 o'clock found me a long way from home. By noon I figured I had gone about 10 miles. The country became more rugged with hills and canyons that made progress slow. The mountain itself seemed as far away as it had in the morning. Distances are very deceiving in the clear air of the North Country.

Shortly before sundown I looked around for a likely place to camp for the night. Baldy was still quite a way off and it would probably take the better part of another day of good hard walking to reach my destination.

Among a clump of young spruce trees I found an excellent place to make a camp for the night. For supper that evening I enjoyed caribou steak cut into strips and held over the flame on a stick until the fat sizzled into the fire. I still had a little coffee left from my evening meal. It was very much diluted, but at least it was warm and relished to the last drop.

During the next forenoon I entered a long winding valley that ran all the way to the foot of the mountain. Anxious to get to Baldy before dark, I stopped only briefly at noon for a bit of cold meat and continued on my way until shortly before sundown, when I arrived at the foot of the mountain.

It was too late to attempt climbing to the top. I had almost decided to make my camp in a nearby thicket when I discovered something that looked like the top of a log cabin protruding from the snow. It didn't take long to get to it for a closer inspection. It proved to be a cabin all right, with snow piled high around it so only the top of the door was visible.

I was so excited over my discovery that I forgot all about making camp. I leaned the rifle against the tree and threw my pack on the snow while I clawed and dug with my mittened hands to get the snow away from the door. It proved to be quite a job, for the snow was packed solid and some of the harder layers had to be cut out in blocks with my hunting knife.

Darkness came before the task was finished. However, I continued working until the door swung open to my tugging upon the latch. It was impossible to see anything inside without a light, but a sickening odor of mildew and rot came through the opening.

Gathering firewood, I quickly built a campfire right outside the open door so the light from the flame would shine inside the cabin. Then cautiously I stepped over the threshold, into the mysterious interior, expecting any moment to stumble over the body of some former occupant who might have lived and died there. Dark forms lying about on the cabin floor proved to be heavy clothing and a rotten caribou skin that fell apart at the touch of my boot. The place gave me a spooky, eerie feeling, and beside, it was just too smelly for me to sleep there. So I decided to spend the night outside by the fire and do further inspecting by the light of day.

I knew there was nothing to be afraid of in the cabin, yet I had that scary feeling we get sometimes when we had just as soon be somewhere else until daylight. All through the night I twisted and turned in the sleeping bag, sticking my head out to look around at the slightest falling of a twig or the rustling of the night wind in the trees. When sleep finally overtook me, I slept so soundly it was daylight before I woke up with the sun shining over the treetops to the south.

Strange how differently things look in the light of day. The cabin wasn't as sinister or mysterious as it had been in the darkness of the evening before. It was just an old cabin to be explored and wondered about. Perhaps it would be a good dry place for the next night's sleep.

After breakfast I explored it. The interior looked a good deal like my own cabin except that the floor had been dug down into the earth about a foot, and one had to step down when entering. It had a well-made fireplace, with an iron rod over the fire to hang pots and things on. The last fire must have been very hot, made from perfectly dry wood, for it had burned out completely into a fine ash that crumbled at the touch.

On the stone hearth stood a cook pot half filled with something that in its time probably was meat but was now a hairy mess of mildew.

What intrigued me most was an old calendar hanging on the wall. Most of the printing had been destroyed by dampness but one of the small pages was fairly well intact and I could make out February 1900. The 10th of that month had been marked with an "X," and there was something scribbled on the margin that was unreadable.

On the bottom of the cardboard were two names, "Sigvart" and "Ana," the last name also unreadable. On the back of the calendar were the names Poulson and Mac, with a lot of figures and check marks that to me suggested the tally of a card game. Evidently two men, either trappers or prospectors, had spent the winter here.

On a small table made from the boards of a packing case were the remnants of a meal on two tin plates. The knives and forks were too rusty for use. A homemade cribbage board and several small figures of bears and dogs were crudely carved in wood.

What had once been a double bed was now a mass of rotting sticks and remnants of a blanket or two were covered with what looked like dog hair.

In one corner was a small keg filled with sand, probably containing fine gold to be cleaned out with quicksilver. Beside it there was a box with 35 rounds of heavy ammunition that wouldn't fit my Krag.

On the rough mantlepiece over the fireplace was the picture of an attractive woman, a couple of wood carvings and a discarded snuffbox containing about two ounces of placer gold, most of it about the size of pinheads. This latter discovery was indeed interesting to me. Come spring, I would certainly be back in this part of the woods to have a good look around.

Kicking around in the debris on the floor, I found what was left of two books, one evidently some sort of a doctor's book and the other a book of poems. I also found a broken runner from a dog sled, pieces of dog harness and a couple of rusty traps.

The Bible says that all good things come from above, but I wasn't exactly thinking about that when I casually glanced above me at the rafters in the cabin. There, suspended from the beams on rawhide straps, I saw a pair of skis, several pairs of woolen mittens, a pair of boots and a pair of "tin pants" such as loggers wore in the Northwest. The tin pants are made from heavy waterproof canvas, so stiff that they can almost stand alone.

If I had prayed for some of the things that I needed most, the items in my discovery would surely have been an answer to my prayer. The skis in particular would fill a great need in my daily life. Without them I would have to wait for the snow to pack hard enough to hold my weight before I could go anywhere, but with skis I could travel anywhere I pleased. Back in Norway I had learned to ski at a very tender age.

Taking the skis down from the beams for a closer inspection, I found them to be a bit warped but usable. With a little work they could be sprung back into shape again. The leather bindings were rotted but that presented no problem because I could easily make new ones from pieces of caribou skin.

The boots didn't look like much at first glance. The bottom parts were made of something like rubber but the tops were leather. They were all wrinkled and seemingly unusable but I decided to take them along with me anyway. I might be able to restore them.

The mittens were no doubt made of very good wool and certainly would have come in handy, but they fell apart from rot when I tried them on.

The indestructible "tin pants" lived up to their reputation and would give me much useful wear in the months to come. They went into my pack with the rest of the unexpected loot.

While browsing around inside this house of mystery I speculated as to what had happened to the former occupants. Why were the meals left half eaten? Why were the cooking utensils left in the cabin? And why the ammunition? And who would leave about $50 worth of fine gold sitting on the mantlepiece? It just didn't add up right. When and if I got back to Nome, I would report my discovery.

Now I turned my attention to the big task that I had come here for, to climb to the top of "Little Baldy." Mentally I had changed the name of the mountain since it wasn't nearly as big as it had looked from a distance.

Leaving my things at the cabin, I swung the rifle over my shoulder and headed up over the tree-covered slope. The going was easy until I got above the timber line, when the climb became more treacherous. Here the wind had polished the snow until it was more like white ice that sent me sprawling every time I got a bit reckless. After about two hours I stood on top of the heap, puffing from exhaustion, but one look around told me why the climb was well worth the trouble.

From the top of Baldy I could see perhaps 50 miles in every direction. It was a wonderful panorama of wilderness beauty. To the north a dark row of hills ran in an east-west direction which I took to be the foothills of the Brooks Range. The hill on which I was standing appeared to be part of a watershed with some valleys bending toward the south and others swinging to the north.

Lingering on for a few last moments, I watched the sun slipping down toward the rim of the horizon, bathing the endless tundra in a glow of pink and purple. Below me the shades of night were slowly creeping over the forest and to the east the first stars were appearing in the sky.

Time to get going. Darkness caught up with me before I reached the bottom, and it was quite a job finding my way back to the camping ground by the old cabin.

There, by the light of the campfire, I worked on the ski bindings and got them in temporary workable shape for the homeward journey. The stars were so bright it was almost like moonlight on the white snow and there would be no trouble finding my way. I could even see the blazes made in the trees more than a hundred yards away.

It didn't take me long to get ready, and with all my belongings strapped on my back, I started out. The skis made a wonderful change from walking on the snow and I made excellent time gliding along, my arms swinging in rhythmic motion with the movement of my body. The trip was uneventful and I reached home late in the afternoon.

I kept my supply of meat hanging on a pole in a spruce thicket right back of the cabin, and stepping out early the next morning to get myself a chunk of fresh meat for dinner, I really got a surprise. My choicest hindquarter was missing and the rest of the meat was lying about on the snow. Bears were hibernating at this time of the year and for a while I just couldn't figure out what sort of animal would be strong enough to carry off a chunk of frozen meat weighing at least 25 pounds.

I felt certain that it was not the work of wolves, and looking around on the snow, I found strange tracks that were neither that of a bear nor a wolf. It was a peculiar track, such as I had never seen before. Whatever it was had dragged the meat over the snow for about 400 feet into the thicket, and there I found what little was left of the meat.

I had plenty of meat and didn't begrudge the thief a feast as long as he didn't make a practice of it. On the other hand, I was bursting with curiosity to find out what this four-legged meat-stealer looked like, for the tracks he left behind fitted no description that I knew of.

I hung the meat back up on a stout pole that would fall against the top of the cabin and wake me up if anybody touched the meat. Secure in my superior wisdom, I settled back into the daily routine of cabin life and soon forgot all about the intruder. Little did I know that I was up against the brainiest marauder in the Northland, the wolverine, who surely would be back for more whenever hunger stirred him to fresh adventures.

About 10 days passed. I came out one morning to do some wood cutting. Glancing over to where the meat hung, I stopped in my tracks. Another chunk of my best meat had disappeared. How, without springing my well-set trap? Upon closer inspection I discovered the rawhide strap holding the meat in place to the pole had been chewed off on top, letting the meat down onto the snow without setting off my burglar alarm.

My wood chopping program for the morning was forgotten. Grabbing my rifle, I set out in pursuit of the culprit, determined to follow the trail left in the snow until I ran him down. But the trail, like the one on the previous visit, ended in a few well-chewed bones.

This was a challenge I couldn't afford to lose, a matching of wits, and I bet the rascal was laughing at my efforts to catch him.

The game finally came to an end one moonlit night. I had just gone to sleep when the burglar alarm went off. The log hit the roof  with a hollow thud that had me wide awake instantly. Jumping out into the snow in my underwear and bare feet, I fired a shot at the fleeing animal and brought him down upon the snow.

With the temperature at 10 below zero, I hurried back inside the cabin where I spent the next half hour rubbing blood circulation back into my bare feet. Later I skinned the animal and used the soft fur to form the upper part of a parka.

For a while I kept a sharp lookout in case the wolverine should have relatives lurking around the location but I never saw another one of that breed all winter. He must have been a bachelor on the prowl.

Spring Was in the Air 10

The month was March, and although it was still cold and snowy on the outside, there was spring in my heart for I knew that I was winning the grim game of survival. The new-found skis played no small part in the spiritual uplift. Most of my daylight hours were spent skiing around the hills near the cabin. I never had so much fun since my school days back in Norway.

On one of my skiing trips I ran into a large flock of ptamigan. They are quite similar to prairie chickens, brown in summer and white in winter, and quite common to the north countries. Being very poor fliers, they fall prey to wolves and foxes, which was probably the reason I had not seen any of them around earlier in the season.

I couldn't afford to use up ammunition on such small fry but I managed to kill four birds by throwing chunks of wood at them. Roasted over the fire, the ptarmigan were a delicious change from my diet of bear and caribou—by this time getting a bit tiresome.

The birds tasted good, all right, but my stomach must have thought otherwise. I woke up in the night with a terrible stomach ache and diarrhea. I lost my appetite for ptarmigan after that. As if to taunt me, several flocks of them came pecking around my cabin that spring, almost as tame as barnyard chickens.

Before winter was over, the thermometer was down to 30 and 35 below zero a couple of times. When I tried to scrape some snow off the thermometer one morning, the glass broke in my hand. It was like losing a friend, a companion of the long winter, and I stood there clutching the thing for several moments before tossing it into the snow.

With the coming of April there was an unmistakable feeling of spring in the air. It was still rather cold at times, especially at night, but the great drifts of snow that had piled up through winter storms took on a tired look. Tree stumps I hadn't seen for months appeared again.

One day in the latter part of April I was chopping wood outside the cabin when I heard dogs barking. At first I took it to be wolves or foxes, but it came again, time after time and louder on the clear air, until there was no mistaking it. It was dogs.

Sticking the ax into the nearest stump I fastened on my skis and set off in the direction of the sound. The snow was sticky and the progress slow, up one hill and down the other, my eyes glued on the distant landscape, always hoping that around the next turn or over the next hill I would actually see people, human beings like myself, somebody to talk to.

About half a mile from the cabin I came across sled tracks and the footprints of two men, one walking behind the sled and the other alongside. Judging from the depth of the runners in the snow, the sled must have been very heavily loaded and headed in an easterly direction.

Pushing my skis along as fast as I could, I caught sight of the men from the top of the ridge. They seemed to be a good two miles ahead and going at a smart clip. I lost them as their team swung in among some little hills and disappeared from view. Like a bloodhound I followed the tracks until one of the rotten ski bindings broke, making the skis useless. Frustrated but unwilling to give up the chase, I stuck the skis into a snowbank and continued on foot, running at a dogtrot in the sled tracks.

After a couple of hours of intermittent walking and running, I could go no farther. Dead tired and puffing like a steam engine, I threw myself down upon the snow to rest. The sun was getting low over the western horizon and there was about an hour of daylight left, so I decided to give up the chase. It was a very hard decision to make, but I had left my rifle and matches in the cabin and had no wish to get caught at night so far from home.

Leaning against a windfall, my eyes followed the trail of the dog team to where it faded into the night shadows already gathering over the forest. It was heartbreaking to be so close and yet miss the opportunity to see and speak to a fellow human being. Only those few who have lived alone under similar circumstances can understand the great emotional strain I felt and the tears of frustration in my eyes.

With a last look at the sled trail, I turned and headed back to the cabin. Hungry and beaten, I arrived about midnight. The fire on the hearth had gone out for the first time since the previous October, and the place felt like an icehouse. However, it didn't take me long to get the fire going and supper cooking.

While eating my belated supper, I pondered on who the men might be—prospectors, trappers or maybe freighters hauling supplies to the Interior while the snow was still on the ground. Anyway, I reasoned with myself, maybe it was for the best that I didn't get to meet them. I might not have liked them.

The breakup of winter came with a rush. It started with a drizzling rain that lasted for several days, turning the snow into a slushy mess. Giant drifts, piled up during the winter storms, receded into the ground so fast that in a few days' time stumps, logs and even spots of bare ground began showing.

The creek, too, came to life. Water ran over the snow until it washed the ice and slush downstream with a great burst, flooding the valley from bank to bank with a grinding, tumbling mass of ice, wood and other debris.

This was the moment I had been waiting for all through the long winter. It was my time to act, too. As soon as the creek water receded enough so I could work along the bank, I was at it from morning to night with pick, shovel and gold pan, testing the half-frozen gravel for signs of color.

At first the frost was a bother, but little by little the water running over the gravel and the warmth of the spring sun combined to thaw the gravel bed so it could be worked.

June brought excellent weather and also daylight all through the night, making it possible to work long hours. I got an occasional pinhead of gold in the pan, but nothing that gave any hope of a strike.

Later, as I grew wiser in the art of prospecting, I suspected I probably had had hundreds of dollars in my hands, but in my ignorance had thrown it away. I often found on the bottom of the pan a grayish-looking stone or what I took to be stone. Consequently I just dumped it out of the pan with the rest of the worthless gravel and sand.

Out of curiosity, I saved a couple of pieces of the stuff and kept it in my pocket for more than a year. It was a shock when a saloon keeper in Nome offered me $80 for my souvenirs. It was then I learned I had been throwing away platinum worth many times the price of gold.

For about three weeks I worked the ground around the cabin without any luck, then I decided to leave this section and continue eastward. On the evening of June 15 I ate my last supper in the cabin that had been my home all through the long winter. It had become a part of my life and it was hard to walk away from.

With the pack on my back and the rifle over my shoulder, I stood inside the open door having a last look at my winter home. It was like saying good-by to a true and proven friend. On the table I left a note, weighed down with a stone, telling whoever might come there about my lonely winter and my dreams.

I put the skis on the rafters. Some future traveler might use them and the bed with the well-crushed spruce boughs, the table and my good old chair that had served me so well.

The fireplace was slowly burning itself out. Turning quickly, I stepped outside, shut the door and placed a small log against it to prevent the wind or a bear from pushing it open. Then I headed up the valley without a backward look.

For the next few days I prospected the country around Little Baldy. The country seemed different, now that the snow was gone. Young grass and moss were growing everywhere, a veritable paradise for game, of which I saw plenty.

I didn't kill any, because I found the creeks loaded with fish that I learned (after many failures) to spear with a sharp stick. I roasted the fish on a stick over the fire and ate them with my fingers.

However, my prospector's luck was not so good. All I found in my gold pan after hundreds of test holes were a few pinhead colors.

Over the hill I went, into another valley and another creek, only to find the same poor results from my hard work. My hands became calloused and sore from swinging the pick and shoveling gravel. My back ached until it was a real effort to crawl out of my blankets each morning.

Traveling east over swamps and muskegs, I crossed numerous smaller creeks until I came to a branch of the Koyukuk, or it might have been the main river itself, for my map was crude and far from accurate. This river proved too deep to wade across. I tried it several times, but on my last attempt I stepped into deep water and the current tumbled me and my pack over and over, nearly drowning me before I reached a row of rocks sticking out of the river.

Clinging to the rocks while getting my breath and my bearings, I discovered that my feet barely touched the bottom while the current gurgled around my head. Somehow, one's brain reacts quickly to such emergencies, and with a couple of swift strokes I swam back to shallow ground and scrambled upon the shore.

Soaking wet and trembling from the cold water and exhaustion, I hurriedly made a campfire to get dried out. Still, I had to laugh at my predicament, I was standing there naked as Adam, warming my rear against the fire while a swarm of mosquitoes attacked my frontside and my clothes dripped on a nearby limb.

The following morning I made myself a small raft, and using the shovel for a paddle, crossed the river without much trouble. The current carried me a mile downstream before I made a safe landing on the other shore.

The mosquitoes got worse as the days warmed. As I panned beside the creeks along the way, the backs of my hands would be covered with them. Slapping at them did no good; they came right back for another drink of Norwegian blood. I tried using the old remedy of smearing soot and grease on my face and neck, and that eased them off a bit, although I could never quite decide which was the most uncomfortable, the sticky mess or the mosquitoes.

It was now daylight all through the night and one evening while camping on a high ridge overlooking the gently rolling hills, I saw the sun shine without setting. It meant I was north of the Arctic Circle, and the midnight sun reminded me of my home in Norway. There being no mosquitoes at this higher elevation, I lay there for a long time reminiscing while I looked at the sun, a red ball of fire that hung in the sky barely over the hilltops. Finally my eyelids grew heavy, and I fell asleep on top of the blankets with my clothes and boots on.

Bonanza   11

Ragged, dirty and slightly discouraged, I wandered over the hills in search of my bonanza. With the pack on my back containing only a few pounds of dried meat and sometimes a fish or two caught along the way, my mind was slowly turning to thoughts of the Outside and a more pleasant way of living.

On the evening of July 4, dead tired from walking all day, I came to the mouth of a narrow valley running in a north-south direction. This valley appeared to be about 10 miles long, with a bluish haze hanging over the upper end. It was about a quarter of a mile wide, with steep rocky sides and rimrock hanging along the top edges. A creek ran through the middle of it, with small green trees growing almost to the water's edge.

Pack on the ground, leaning on my rifle barrel, I stood there in the evening calm, looking up the valley where the last rays of the setting sun painted the rimrocks crimson and the shadows of night gathered on the lower ground.

I should have made camp for the night right there, but I had a strange feeling that something was about to happen, a premonition of things to come. I decided I just had to investigate the place, tired or not.

Slinging the pack on my back and the rifle over my sore shoulder, I headed up the valley, determined to see the length of it before turning in. I hadn't eaten since noon, but like a homing salmon heading for the spawning grounds I followed that unexplained urge, pushing on through the Arctic summer night.

About midnight I reached the upper end of the valley, where the creek disappeared from sight around a bend through a narrow canyon with perpendicular rocky cliffs.

Too tired to stagger any farther, I found a place to bed down and unrolled my blankets beneath a spruce tree about 100 feet from the creek. I sat on the blankets trying to eat something but my weary body could take no more. I tumbled over and went to sleep, clutching a piece of meat in my fingers.

In a few hours I was awake again, just as the sun came peeking over the rim of hills in the northeast. Trembling from weariness, I crawled out of the blankets, built a small campfire and hung the coffeepot full of water over the coals. Although I had no coffee to put in it, a hot drink in the morning always gave me a lift.

While waiting for the water to get hot I picked up the gold pan and went down to the creek for my morning swim. Peeling off my clothes, I jumped into a deep hole in the creek and swam with the water splashing about me. At first it felt like I had been stabbed, the water was so cold. My body turned red from blood coming to the surface but after a few minutes I got used to the water and enjoyed it immensely.

My water frolic was suddenly interrupted by a nearby sneeze. Not having seen anybody for so long a time, I looked around in great surprise. I found the source but it was not another prospector as I had expected. A fat hunk of a black bear stood on his haunches in the brush less than 20 feet away. He probably had never seen a human being before, and from the funny look on his face he appeared more startled than I was.

Moving on his hind legs close to the edge of the water, he stood with eyes blinking, turning his head from side to side like a man in deep thought over what he saw. For several minutes he watched while I swam around, splashing the water toward him, until finally he had enough and ambled off into the brush grunting to himself.

By this time I had had enough of the cold water, too, and climbed out on the bank, drying myself on my shirt after which I wrung it out and put it on. A man can't have everything and I had no towels.

The water in the pot was still boiling, so chewing on a piece of meat I scanned the creekbank for a likely place to try my luck with the pan. I found such a place a couple of hundred feet upstream from my swimming hole. The creek was shallow at this point, only about a foot deep, with a gently flowing current and fat trout dashing around in the crystal-clear water.

Running along the bank of the creek there was a layer of reddish-rusty gravel that looked good to me. I dug the pick into it and filled the pan. On my knees beside the creek I began washing it out as I had done a thousand times before. It was just another pan, just another of many tests, and I expected nothing unusual to happen.

Whistling while I worked, I turned the pan gently so the water would run over the edge and wash away the lighter dirt and gravel until I had only a handful of black sand left in the bottom. Dipping a little clean water into the pan, I tilted it gently.

There shining in the morning sun, were hundreds of tiny yellow specks and *a nugget as big as my little finger!*

Grasping the nugget in my fingers, I dropped the pan and ran up and down beside the creek yelling like a madman.

"GOLD! I'VE STRUCK IT!"

I felt as though someone had opened the First National Bank and told me to help myself.

It took a while to regain self-control. The pent-up emotions of a year of fruitless search had come to such a sudden end that now I laughed and cried at the same time.

My campfire burned out; my breakfast was forgotten. On my knees beside the creek I dug and panned hour after hour, all through the day, without stopping to eat or rest.

About 11 o'clock the sun went down over the hills to the northwest. Shortly afterwards I passed out and collapsed on the gravel bar from hunger and exhaustion. When I came to, my head was swimming and my body was aching from head to foot. I lay there for a long time, rubbing circulation into legs that felt dead from my having been on my knees all day.

Back on wobbly legs, I gathered my day's work together. I estimated it to be worth around $2,000, mostly in the size of small beans and match heads. All the fine gold that my shaky fingers couldn't pick out of the pan, I just dumped back on the ground. It is funny how one changes with prevailing circumstances.

With the gold in my hands, and laughing like a fool, I stumbled across the gravel to my camping ground. There I spread the gold out on top of my blankets, where I could enjoy watching it glitter while I ate dry caribou meat.

67

With my appetite satisfied, I lit my pipe. The tobacco sack was long since empty but I had found a fairly good substitute for tobacco in caribou moss and birch bark rubbed very fine. It smoked after a fashion but had a vicious bite. Every time I finished a pipeful, I had to stick my tongue out and wring it to remove the sting.

With my back against a birch tree, I sat there puffing and looking down over the valley. I was king of my valley and no king could ever have known a happier moment!

As the days went by, I realized that working with the pan was much too slow. I needed a sluice box, now that I had found a pay streak, to clean the gold out of the gravel. It would require at least three wide boards and some smaller pieces of lumber to make the riffles inside the box. I looked for the biggest trees along the creek, trees that when flattened on one side would provide a surface of at least 10 inches in width and 16 feet or more in length.

All the tools available for the undertaking were the ax and my knife, not much perhaps, but sufficient for a man with a will (and of that the Lord had given me a plentiful supply). With the ax filed to razor's edge, and after hunting all over the place, by noon I had knocked down three spruce trees that I felt would provide the needed boards.

For the next three days the chips flew as I flattened one side of each tree. They became the funniest-looking "boards" you could imagine, but with one flat surface on each I could make a usable sluice box, which is only three boards nailed together to form a trough.

Inside, crossways on the bottom, there are riffles made from small pieces of wood about four inches in height. They are placed about six inches apart, slanting gently upstream to catch the fine black sand and gold being washed through. The gravel is shoveled into the upper end of the box and the water carries the dirt and gravel down the length of it, discharging the waste at the lower end. Being much heavier, the gold and black sand sink behind the riffles and are cleaned up with the pan every few days.

After four days of work with ax and knife, I had the sluice box finished and placed in position in the creek. It was a clumsy-looking thing to say the least. The inside of the box was about as smooth as I could get it, but the outside was half round with the bark still on. Of course I had no nails to hold the boards together, but wooden pegs took care of that and they worked, which after all, was the main thing. Now, after a few adjustments to get it set at a proper angle so the water would flow through at the right speed, I was ready to go.

At noontime on the fourth day, with my hunger satisfied by grayling, I began the tedious job of digging gravel out of the bank and shoveling it into the box. At last I was in production. In a few days my first cleanup would tell me just how rich the gravel bed was.

For the next two days I worked from early morning till late at night, digging and shoveling until the creek had a rusty-brown color as far down as I could see. Once in a while I caught a glimpse of a small nugget glistening in the sun as it tumbled along the riffles to disappear into the bottom of the box. It gave me added assurance that I was indeed in the pay streak.

On the morning of the third day I could stand the suspense no longer. I had to find out how rich I was by this time. Shutting off the water on the upper end, I carefully lifted what had been caught by the riffles out of the sluice box, rinsing all the fine dirt and sand. With the gold pan, I began washing it out as I had seen the miners do in Nome.

I moved the pan gently, with just enough water in it to flush the lighter sediment and sand over the edge, until there was a smear of yellow left along the rim of the pan.

My heart beat like a hammer and sweat ran down my face while my trembling fingers gathered the coarser pieces from the pan. This was the moment I had been dreaming about.

My entire body was trembling from the strain and tension of the moment. This was a moment I would never live again. It comes only once in a prospector's life, that first strike. *And there was no doubt about it by now, it was a real strike!*

It was late at night before I finished the cleanup and had the box ready to continue the sluicing. Picking up the coffeepot in which I put the gold, I staggered over the stony ground to my blankets, peeled off my boots and in a few moments I was sound asleep, clutching the coffeepot in my hands.

For the next couple of weeks or so—I had lost track of time—I worked almost continuously, sometimes all through the night when it was cool, to sleep in the warmth of the sun during daytime. My only break in the routine was time out to catch a few fish in the creek or to gather a few blueberries that were ripening a little way from camp. Once in a while I would stop long enough to watch the antics of a bear and her cubs fishing in the creek above my sluice box. They gave me many a laugh, the mother bear catching fish like the expert she was, and the two young ones trying to emulate mama only to get their snouts full of water and jump back upon the bank sneezing and squealing.

Caribou passed my camp from time to time. They were so tame that sometimes they came within a stone's throw from where I worked, but they gave me only a casual glance. However, my appetite for meat was not very keen, with the abundance of fish to be had in my creek, so I didn't bother them either.

With my riches piling up as the days went by, and my body worn to the breaking point from long hours of hard work, I sometimes found myself leaning on the shovel, daydreaming about the Outside. I dreamed of cities and people, of hotels with clean beds to sleep in, towels for my bath and meals served on white tablecloths. I had to shake myself to get rid of that money-isn't-everything-feeling that was fast sneaking up on me.

Spitting in my hands, I swung into action with the shovel, heaving the gravel into the sluice box while my mind kept nagging to stop this backbreaking work and go south into a better land to enjoy the better things in life.

These sessions with myself pestered me more and more each day, and it became harder each time to convince myself I should stay a little longer and gather just a little more yellow stuff before heading back to civilization.

Finally, one sunny morning in the first part of August, it happened. I was about through cleaning the sluice box, in fact I was washing out the last pan, down on my knees by the creek, when I began thinking about all those pretty girls I had seen in San Francisco. The pan moved slower and slower and suddenly my mind was made up. With a loud whoop I threw the gold pan into the creek and jumped to my feet. I was going back, back to the bright lights and those pretty maidens.

Like a dam burst loose, I hustled about camp getting my things together for the journey. That didn't take long because my clothes were worn out except those I had on, and they were about as dirty as they could get. My pants were so stiff with grime they stood up by themselves whenever I took them off.

I needed something to carry the gold in, something stout enough to hold and protect the heavy metal. The best I could do was to cut the four deep pockets out of my canvas pants. I filled each pocket with gold and tied a string around the top. It seems there is always a solution to every problem if one looks hard enough.

Just in case I might want to come back for more gold, I dragged the sluice box away from the creek where the high water wouldn't take it downstream, and turned it upside down on high ground. Inside I placed my pick, shovel and other odds and ends that I would have no further need for unless I returned. At the moment I could see no reason for returning. I would never go broke again. That was what I thought.

Now that I was ready and packed for the journey, I yanked a few trout from the creek and put them in the pan for a quick dinner. While the fish were sizzling I had a last look around and put up a few markers on the trees around my diggings. These were just blazes on the trees with my name and date, in case somebody else should come along and think I had abandoned the claim. Not that these markers would do any good if a passerby worked the ground. The claim was not registered and I didn't even know how to go about such a procedure. At the moment it didn't bother me. I had all the money I would need, with no worry about tomorrow.

Going Outside 12

I said good-by to my camp and headed off in a westerly direction through the scrubby forest. The sun was in the south so it must have been about noon and I should be able to cover many miles before making camp for the evening.

On my back was the gold, the blankets, the frying pan, a little ammunition for my rifle, strips of dried meat hanging on the outside of the pack and six grayling dangling on a string. With the rifle over my shoulder and the ax in hand with which I blazed trees here and there in case I should ever return—I left my diggings.

Trudging through the scattered forest, I made excellent time. There was hardly any underbrush and the ground was mostly hard and dry. That was good, because my boots were worn so thin I could feel the sharp stones through the soles. However, I was so confident now I think I could have walked barefoot to Nome.

At sundown I made camp in a little birch grove on the edge of a stream, protected from the north winds that had been getting a bit cool lately.

I fried some of the fish and afterwards enjoyed a stout smoke on my old pipe. By this time it was pretty well worn out from my chewing the stem and burning the bowl with my moss-and-bark mixture.

The cool evening seemed especially beautiful with the soft pink of the sunset, the water in the creek chattering over the rocks and, a short distance away, several caribou grazing peacefully in the twilight. I felt a bit sad to be leaving the wilderness I had learned to love. But life is a constant change and like the tide, must have its way.

The next few days passed uneventfully, until the evening of the fourth day. Shortly after sundown I was about to make camp when I spotted a campfire about a mile or so away. It startled me, and I decided not to make my own fire until I had investigated who my neighbors might be. Although I craved to see other human beings, the gold in my pack made me cautious and suspicious.

I slipped a cartridge into the barrel of my rifle and advanced among the trees where I could see without being seen. This worked fine until I was about 300 feet away. Then the barking of a dog broke the stillness of the night. The two men jumped to their feet, silhouettes against the campfire. Like a shadow moving in the darkness, I saw a large dog bearing down on me, fast. I held my rifle ready, not wanting to be chewed by a vicious dog. It turned out to be an unnecessary precaution. The dog, just an oversized pup, jumped all over me, wagging its tail and greeting me like a long-lost friend.

The strangers were ready for trouble too. In the shadows beyond the fire I made out the form of a third man, the glint from the fire shining on his rifle barrel. I surely didn't want to be shot, so I yelled at the top of my voice, "Hello, hello!" My voice seemed strange and hollow in the night. They were my first words spoken to a fellow man in over a year.

Petting the pup still bouncing around me, I approached the campfire where the two men stared in utter disbelief at what they saw—a ragged, unshaven young man with long disheveled hair, appearing out of the brush.

One man by the campfire spoke in Swedish. The third member of the group came closer to the fire, leaned his rifle against a tree and joined his companions in staring at me.

Moving closer into the circle of light, I dropped the pack on the ground and the rifle across the top, then sat down on a log to get my breath while sizing up the situation.

The men were conversing in Swedish, which I could understand if they didn't speak too fast. At the moment they were talking about me and wondering where I had come from. One of them used the word *toki*, which I knew from the old country to mean crazy or out of his mind in Swedish slang.

I guess I did look like a wild man, but to hear them mention it made me grin. One of them, realizing I had understood what he said, grinned back at me.

"Are you Swede?" he asked.

"No," I replied, "I am Norwegian, and a very hungry Norwegian." I looked at the stewpot simmering over the fire. "I haven't eaten since morning and have covered about 40 miles today."

Now that I proved harmless, all three shook hands with me and invited me to share their supper. They asked me a hundred questions (in Swedish) about how I happened to be there. When I told them I had prospected alone and stayed over winter, they were dubious of my tale, wanting to know just where. I supplied the details without mentioning the gold. From my appearance they probably thought I was as poor as a church mouse, and I wanted to keep them thinking that way.

The invitation for supper I gladly accepted. One look at the stewpot made my mouth drool like a fox in a chicken pen. Mixed with the hunks of well-cooked meat were generous pieces of potato, which I hadn't tasted since leaving Nome. I had gotten so used to my simple fare of fried meat, dried meat and half-cooked fish that I had almost forgotten about civilized food and the sight of this concoction nearly overwhelmed me with delight.

In a few minutes we were all squatting on logs around the fire, filling ourselves with the heavenly mixture. None of us had much to say while eating. They were evidently hungry, too, from a hard day's work, and we all ate till we could eat no more. Then putting away the tin plates, the tallest one of the three—who seemed to be the leader of the group—brought out a pouch filled with real tobacco. What a welcome change from the birch bark and caribou moss I had been smoking for months!

Relaxing around the fire, I found that two of the men were Swedish and the third a Finlander. One came from a small town in northern Sweden, only a few hundred miles from my hometown in Norway, which he had visited many times. This gave us much to talk about as fellow Scandinavians, and cemented the friendship of the trail.

The Finlander had come from near the Swedish border and spoke perfect Swedish. Since our English was none too good, we conversed in Swedish which is very similar to Norwegian. We kept a steady flow of conversation going on all imaginable subjects, from world news, on which I was a year and a half behind, to the doings of Klondike Kate.

I found out they were working a placer claim and had an elaborate outfit set up along a creekbank only 100 feet from where we sat. In the darkness I hadn't seen any of their equipment and had thought they were travelers like myself.

One Swede, Carlson, told me they had used two hired dog teams to freight their equipment and supplies to the claim while the spring snow was still on the ground, and that they had intended to stay on until freezeup in the fall before returning to Nome.

Before turning in for the night, Carlson lit an oil lantern and showed me their cabin, built in a spruce thicket to protect it from wind and weather. He also showed me the sluice boxes, a whole string of them made from real sawed lumber, fastened together with nails. This was a millionaire's outfit compared to my single homemade sluice box of rough logs and wooden pegs. But, it also made me feel rather proud of my own accomplishments, that of a lone man with an ax and imagination.

After an inspection of the claim, we had a last cup of coffee by the fire, then the three of them turned in to the bunks in the cabin. I spurned an offer to sleep on the floor, preferring to spend the night under the stars.

Tired from the long trail, I went to sleep the moment I hit the blankets and slept until Carlson, prodding me with the point of his boot, sang out, "Hey, fellow! It's 5 o'clock. Want to have breakfast with us?"

With the mention of breakfast, I was wide awake and on my feet before he could extend a second invitation. For a long time breakfast had meant only a chunk of meat or perhaps a fried fish, with creek water to wash it down. Not that I had any complaints—I was more than thankful for the Lord's mercies—but this, the smell of bacon on the fresh morning air, to hear it sizzling in the pan, was almost like already having one foot in civilization.

The Finn was making breakfast. He was an expert with a stack of hot cakes and thick slices of tasty bacon. They even had butter, syrup and a potful of real coffee, the aroma of it blending to perfection with the rest of his culinary production. After what I had gone through in the past 18 months, I could almost shut my eyes and believe I had died and gone to heaven.

After breakfast I said good-by to my friends and continued on my way westward, enriched by much good advice about the quickest way to Nome, a nice piece of bacon and a big handful of smoking tobacco.

The pup, tied up so he wouldn't follow me, was wagging his tail and yelping farewell as far as I could hear him. It had been a most happy meeting and I whistled as I walked along the creek bound for the Outside.

After two weeks of hard walking I finally arrived at Nome in a driving rainstorm. Soaked to the skin and shivering from the chill air, I entered the first restaurant I came to on Front Street. I was half starved and so tired I could have lain right down on the floor by the potbellied stove and slept the clock around. But I had two important things to do: to satisfy my voracious appetite with all the food I could get my hands on; and next, to get passage on the first ship Outside.

My first quest was easily filled because I was the only customer in the place and the cook was willing and ready to be of service. While that gentleman took my order, I noticed he looked me over in a queer sort of way, as if I were a ghost or something to be afraid of. When he retired to the kitchen to fill the order, I took a quick look at myself in a small wall mirror. What I saw was enough to scare me, too. My face was drawn into a mess of wrinkles, the skin tanned from wind and weather into the color of old leather boots. A dirty-looking scar from frostbite ran down the side of my nose. The hair was matted from neglect and hung like a mop over my ears and neck, both badly in need of soap and water. No wonder the man stared at me.

Such trifles as looks were soon forgotten over a man-sized beef steak—not caribou nor bear this time, but good old cow meat imported from the States and served with a heaping helping of boiled potatoes.

While I ate, the cook informed me that he was the owner of the place. He sat down across from me, leaning his elbows on the oilcloth-covered tabletop. I could tell he was very curious to find out more about me and where I came from, but I parried the questions with plenty of my own. I didn't want to let this fellow or anybody else find out what I carried in my pack.

I did get a bit of information from him that made me swallow the last of the steak in a hurry. He told me there was a freighter leaving for San Francisco at almost any time and that the next regular steamer for Seattle would not arrive for another week or two.

Thanking him for the information, I grabbed a handful of cigars out of the box on the counter and paid my bill with a gold nugget.

Lugging my belongings, I set out to find the captain of the freighter. Luck was with me. I caught up with him in the Northern Commercial store. At first he wouldn't even speak to me, probably taking me for a luckless bum who wanted to get Outside, but here my Norwegian came in handy. In the store there was a Norwegian-American working for the Alaska Steamship Company, the same Petersen who had given me a helping hand in Seattle. He had a talk with the ship's captain who had told me his ship was a freighter that carried no passengers—but now as a favor to Petersen, he would carry me to San Francisco if I were willing to use an empty bunk in the crew's quarters.

Was I willing? Oh, boy!

In one corner of the room, out of sight of the rest of the people, I dug from the bag a small handful of gold that I gave to Petersen, He in turn paid my fare to the captain.

Petersen gave me a lot of much-needed advice about San Francisco, where to cash my gold, and what to do and not to do to avoid falling into the "slicker traps" of the big town. He also gave me a letter of introduction to a bank. I will be forever grateful to that gentleman.

From here things moved fast. There was no time for a bath, a haircut or even to look up my old friend, the Dane, whom I had promised myself to see before leaving Nome. Of course this last item could well be left out, because I only wanted to let him know what he missed by not going with me. On the other hand, if he had seen me at this time, maybe he would have been glad that he didn't, because I surely was a sorry mess of rags and dirt, and didn't look at all prosperous.

My rifle and other odds and ends I left at the store, to be picked up if and when I should return. Shaking hands with Petersen, I rushed off down the street, pack on my back, to catch up with the captain.

Things had happened so fast that it made my head swim, and in less than two hours after arriving in Nome I found myself in a bouncing tugboat on the way to the ship anchored a short distance offshore.

The captain was in a hurry to get out to sea and the crew was standing by when we got aboard, so it was only a matter of minutes to up the anchor and we stood out into the Bering Sea, homeward bound.

Leaning on the rail in the stern of the ship, I watched the city of Nome slowly fade into the mist. To me, it was a year and a half that will live forever in my memory.

A Fool and His Money 13

I was fortunate to be sharing a cubbyhole cabin with the ship's bo's'n, a big rawboned Norwegian who spoke my language well although he had been sailing on the Pacific Coast for many years without getting home to his native land. He told me the ship had just delivered a cargo of dredging equipment to Nome and that they hoped to be able to make yet another trip North before freezeup. I surely wouldn't envy him about returning to the Bering Sea in late fall. It was rough enough now to suit me, with the freighter groaning at the seams with every plunge into the waves.

The cabin had two bunks, an upper and a lower. I slept in the upper one and every time the ship rolled I had to grab for the edge of the bunk and hang on to keep from being tossed out on deck. The bo's'n got a big kick out of watching my acrobatics until I learned to relax and swing with the motion of the old tub.

I used my pack for a pillow, and no one aboard, I am sure, had any idea what riches it contained. The news had gone around from the skipper that Petersen had paid my fare and they all took me to be some hard-luck guy going home to a more secure life in the States.

As the days went by, I made friends with the officers and the crew of the ship. Among the crew were several Scandinavians, Swedes, Norwegians and Danes, with whom I spent many leisure hours talking old country.

They all treated me with the kind sympathy one would show toward a fellowman down on his luck. One of them even told me he would be glad to let me have a few dollars when we got ashore so I could clean up and get myself a job.

I was deeply touched by such a show of kindness, but underneath I chuckled to myself. If they only knew what was in that dirty old pack in my bunk! I rather enjoyed being the poverty-stricken bum, but promised myself I would compensate them for their kind hearts when we reached port.

Our progress south was slow and tedious because of the high wind and rough seas all the way from Nome down to the Aleutian chain, where we crossed into the Pacific Ocean. From there on the going was a good deal better, and the weather warmed up.

The ship was old and made only seven or eight knots. The journey grew monotonous with nothing to do but eat and sleep. Our first landfall was Cape Mendocino on the California coast on the 14th day after leaving Nome.

The following day, about 10 o'clock in the morning, we crawled out of a fog bank to head straight for the Golden Gate and San Francisco. I stood in the bow of the ship watching the busy harbor scene, with ferryboats hustling back and forth across the bay and the buildings of the city growing taller on the green hillsides as we drew near.

Finally we were at the dock and I was a man in a hurry. I shook hands with the captain and the crew, thanking them for the courtesies extended me, then down the gangway I went, pack on my back, ready to face the big town.

There were plenty of cabs, both horse-drawn and motor cabs, along the curb outside the dock, but having no cash with which to pay for such service I decided to walk to the bank to exchange my gold for dollars. It was more of a job than I had expected, because the city was big and the streets were confusing. After a couple of hours of trudging up one street and down another, with sweat trickling down my face, I finally arrived at my destination.

Inside the bank, the man behind the brass grille looked me over with a suspicious eye until I produced the note that Mr. Petersen had given me in Nome. The man read the note and that changed the situation in a hurry. The teller called someone who took me into a private office and shook my hand with the grip he would give a brother returning from the dead. Next, that gentleman offered me a cigar that I gladly accepted and puffed on with great relish, while the employees eyed me through the open door.

The banker turned out to be a human sort of a fellow, once we got down to business, and chatted in a very friendly fashion while he and an assistant weighed the gold and jotted down the amount of each scaleful. He told me that he nearly went to Alaska himself, but he got cold feet. Looking at his spindly physique, I thought he would never have made a success as a prospector anyway.

With the transaction completed and my pockets stuffed with rolls of paper money, I took leave of the house of Mammon to get myself a room at the Palace Hotel, one of San Francisco's finest. The banker in the meantime had called a horse-drawn cab to take me to the hotel in style. Ushering me to the door in person, he had a last word of admonition, to beware of card sharks, thieves and confidence men.

The liveried driver of the cab gave me a look of consternation when I threw that dirty pack ahead of me into the cab and climbed in beside it with a snappy, "To the Palace."

As we drove down the street he suggested that there were many cheaper hotels in the city, and asked if I wouldn't rather go to one of them. He seemed quite happy, though, when at the door of the Palace I tipped him with a $5 bill. He drove off smiling.

Brushing past the doorman with the pack slung over my shoulder, I went right through the middle of the fine lobby before I realized that I didn't exactly fit in with the elegant patronage of the place. Heads turned as I continued to make my way toward the desk, and one man actually held his nose with the gesture of being overcome with the aroma of dead caribou still clinging to my unwashed clothes.

At the desk the clerk stared at me with open-mouthed disbelief. He backed away muttering, "No room," while his hands flayed the air with that get-out-of-here motion.

The situation was very embarrassing. People sitting around the lobby turned in their chairs for a better look at the spectacle taking place at the desk.

Jabbering away in my broken English, I tried to tell the clerk that I had come from Alaska and had plenty of money to pay my way. In an effort to convince him, I dug from my pocket a handful of $100 bills. They fell from my now trembling hands and scattered on the lobby floor. To make it worse, when I bent to pick them up, bundles of money fell out of my back pockets, too.

On hands and knees I gathered up my wealth, so embarrassed that I just wanted to get up and run out of the place, when for the first time in my young life, I heard money talk.

It was, perhaps, the sight of so much ready cash together with my mention of the magic word Alaska, that did the trick. When I got to my feet, a man that I later came to know as the assistant manager, confronted me with a broad smile and his hand outstretched.

"Welcome to San Francisco, Sir!" With a gentle hand upon my shoulder, he steered me to the desk where the clerk already had the book open and ready for my registry.

Now that my entry into the sacred confines of the hotel had been verified by higher authority the clerk, with a broad grin on his face, inquired, "How many rooms would you like, Sir?"

How many? For a moment I didn't know what to say. Just so I wouldn't offend anybody, I took a chance on two and replied, "Two rooms with bath."

Two bellboys took over, hustling me and my dirty pack to the brass-grilled elevator and upstairs.

My two rooms were filled with all the elegance and conveniences of that day. Best of all, my two bathrooms were supplied with plenty of good-smelling soap, ready for me to wash Alaska off my dirty carcass.

The bellboys, each with a silver dollar in hand, assured me that anything I should want would be mine at a moment's notice. I promptly asked for a barber and a supply of the best cigars to be had in the hotel.

For a few minutes after the bellboys left I wandered about my little palace, taking in the bathrooms that smelled with the fresh fragrance of soap, the soft beds and chairs and the front windows from which I had a perfect view of wide, hustling Market Street below.

Such things as anyone today might take for granted and hardly see at all were to me a revelation of beauty, comfort and all the things that I had dreamed about, suddenly come true. For 17 months I had not had a hot bath, only a quick wash-off in cold creek water with little or no soap, and now I had all these things at my fingertips, ready to be enjoyed as I wished. I had to pinch myself to make sure it was real.

Pulling off my dirty clothes that I had worn so long, I took a look in the mirror. My face and neck were wind-burned to a brown crisp, giving away at the neckline of my underwear to a body of dirty-white that hadn't been exposed to the sunshine for a long time. A fuzzy crop of whiskers clung to my chin.

A knock on the door and the bellboys entered with the cigars. A waiter brought a delicious meal. Aladdin's lamp was really working.

Before the meal was finished, the barber arrived. He threw a sheet around my nakedness and quickly took care of my tonsorial needs. It was all too wonderful, this transformation from a dirty, weather-beaten prospector to a civilized gentleman.

Alone again in the room, I began the main event that I had been looking forward to more than anything else, the bath. For the next two hours I enjoyed myself immensely, soaking Alaska out of my system while singing at the top of my voice.

When I came out of the tub I remembered I had thrown all of my clothes into the wastebasket because I did not want to wear the dirty things again. Something had to be done fast. A call to the desk brought all my needs up to the room in no time.

Two tailors, with measuring tapes around their necks, came trooping in, followed by a couple of bellboys carrying clothing and boxes filled with everything that a gentleman should need. There were shirts of silk and shirts of cotton, undergarments, socks, shoes, ties, hats and six suits all guaranteed to fit me with a little alteration here and there.

I stood in the middle of the floor, hanging on to a towel wrapped around my midsection, while one of the men hunted through the boxes for a pair of shorts that would fit me. His companion in the meantime measured me lengthwise and crosswise with the tape.

For the tailors it must have been a trying two hours, but I had to agree with them, looking in the mirror, that they had done their job well. I was dressed in a natty double-breasted gray suit that fitted me to perfection; pearl-gray button shoes, the rage of the day; a polka-dot tie and, to top it off, a fedora set at a jaunty angle on my head. I was really a dude now, dressed fit to kill.

When I went down to the lobby, nobody paid any attention because I looked just as elegant as the best of them and (to my notion) even a bit better than most. The assistant manager who had greeted me upon my arrival came across the lobby to shake hands and wish me happiness in the city. The clerk and the bellboys called me "Sir" and treated me with the respect and courtesy accorded a moneyed gentleman.

It all struck me as quite funny, what a few good rags would do for a man in this cockeyed civilization. Only this morning no one would accord me a pleasant look, and now my slightest wish was fulfilled with a bow and a "Yes, Sir." I probably would be able to stand it for a while, but it was all so painfully artificial, with none of the warmth I was used to in the North.

Strolling around the streets near the hotel, I remembered the men aboard the ship. They had been very good to me on the way down from Nome and I thought it would be a good idea to go down there and perhaps take the whole lot of them out for dinner.

Getting into a horse-drawn cab in front of the hotel, I told the driver to take me to the waterfront in hopes that I could find the dock where the ship was moored. I had been in such a hurry to get uptown that morning, I hadn't paid much attention to the streets nor landmarks that I passed, but the driver assured me that he would find the ship all right.

We set off at a frisky trot down the cobblestone street toward the waterfront, the driver threading his way in and out among the late afternoon traffic of horse-drawn wagons, cabs and quite a number of automobiles. It was all a wonderful experience, riding along like a gentleman over the same streets that only that morning I had covered on foot with the pack on my back.

The waterfront was a beehive of activity with ships from many nations and of all descriptions loading and unloading cargo. There were steamships, sailing schooners, square-riggers that had come around the Horn bringing machinery and textiles from the East Coast, and squat lumber schooners from Washington and Oregon.

Searching from one dock to another, I found the ship and dismissed the cab. Aboard the ship the crew and longshoremen were already busy stowing away cargo for the next trip North. None of them paid any attention to me as I made my way along the cluttered deck to where the captain and the bo's'n were standing. Neither of the two men recognized me at first, but when I spoke the bo's'n, with a wide grin on his face, blurted out, "What did you do, kid, rob a bank?"

The captain, looking me over from head to foot, joined in: "I wouldn't have believed it if I hadn't seen it with my own eyes."

For a few moments they both seemed speechless at the change that had taken place. They just stood there looking and grinning, then opened up with a barrage of questions that all amounted to the same thing, "Where did you get the money?"

Well, I had to tell them a bit of my story, that I had been one of the lucky ones in Alaska and the old packsack that I had used for a pillow in my bunk on the ship was heavy with gold.

One by one the crew members realized who I was, and slipped away from their duties of loading long enough to come over and shake hands and gaze at the bum turned dude.

I visited aboard the ship for an hour or two, then wound up by inviting the officers and the entire crew to dinner uptown that evening. The invitation was accepted with happy anticipation and much embarrassing backslapping by the sailors, who eagerly looked forward to an evening on the town with all the trimmings that money could buy. I promised them a party they would long remember.

At 7 that evening, four automobiles with liveried chauffeurs loaded all the crew that could be spared from duty. They pulled up in front of the Argosy Club, where I had engaged a private dining room for the occasion. The doorman received them with eyebrows a bit askew, for although they were dressed in their Sunday best, the manners and language of this happy crowd were not exactly compatible with the usual clientele of the club with the golden doorknob. But, once inside, they were left pretty much to themselves, to enjoy the seven-course dinner washed down with vintage champagne, amid boisterous conversation and laughter.

Adding to the evening's fun was a three-piece string orchestra that played during the dinner, while six dancing girls whirled about, to the delight of the enthusiastic sailors.

Not being a drinking man myself, I think I had more fun out of the evening's performance than any of the rest of the group, and it certainly was a fitting climax to my year-and-a-half of loneliness in the Far North.

About 4 in the morning the party broke up and I saw them safely aboard the ship. I had paid my debt in gratitude and I am sure I gave them much to talk about on the long journey back to Nome.

My first day in San Francisco had been a hectic one and dead tired, I tumbled into bed in the hotel for my first night's sleep in a civilized environment for a long, long time.

The next day, well rested and raring to go, I set about to fulfill my ambition in America, the one I had been dreaming of by my Alaska campfires. I wanted to marry some nice American girl, get into some kind of business and become a good American. But how to go about acquiring all this? I had not the faintest idea. But, being a young man with a direct approach to my problems, I did the only thing that came to mind.

Dressed in all my finery, with pocketfuls of money, I stood in front of the hotel watching the girls go by—blondes, brunettes and redheads. They were all so beautiful it was hard to make up my mind, but whenever I saw one that took my particular fancy, I would step out and tip my hat with a pleasant "Good morning, Miss."

Instead of stopping they only gave me a startled look and hurried up the street. I tried this approach for a couple of days, but never got to first base and gave it up as a bad idea.

On the third day I went to an afternoon show at the California Theatre, where they had a very fine orchestra and 20 girls performing on the stage, dancing and singing. I enjoyed it so much that I went back for the evening performance too. After the show I met the orchestra leader in the lobby of the theater and we got to talking. In my broken English I told him how much I liked the music.

When he found that I had come from Alaska, he became especially interested. He said his father had gone to Alaska some years before and had probably struck bad luck in the territory, because he never came home again.

The leader of the orchestra seemed to be such a fine fellow I invited him and entire troupe to come to the hotel the following night after the show, for a get-acquainted party. He accepted the invitation. I walked back to the Palace in a happy mood, having enjoyed a good show and also having a chance to improve my English conversing with a gentleman.

Now as you read this, you might take me to be some sort of a screwball (putting it in modern English) but to me it made sense. My English being very limited, people had trouble understanding what I meant, so I used a more direct approach to get what I wanted.

Most immigrants like to forget their early years in America, the "Greenhorn Years" and the boners they pulled because of being unfamiliar with the ways of Americans and the English language. To me, these years were wonderful and full of meaning, although many times I have had to laugh at my own clumsiness in this regard.

Late in the evening of the day following my visit to the theater I sat in my suite, puffing on a cigar while trying to read the *Evening Chronicle*. I had forgotten all about my invitation to the show people and it must have been close to midnight when I heard a knock on my door and lots of voices in the hallway.

Surprised, I laid aside the newspaper and went to the door in my stocking feet to see what it was all about, I wasn't left in doubt for long. Leading the bevy of about 20 hungry show people was my orchestra leader friend of the day before, followed by a group of wriggling, laughing show girls, pouring through the door like the incoming tide until both of my rooms were filled to overflowing.

For a few moments I stood there flabbergasted. I knew I had invited them, but now that they were here, what in the world would I do with them?

The orchestra leader laughingly came to my rescue, suggesting food and drinks. A call to the office did the rest.

With typical Palace efficiency, the order appeared like magic. In minutes the card tables were set up in both of my rooms, loaded with food and champagne, enough of the latter to take a bath in, as some of them suggested.

I never touched liquor in my life and still don't, but my guests seemed to enjoy themselves swigging down the stuff until the early morning hours. By daylight most of them had toppled off to sleep wherever they could find a place to lie down, and I had to get myself another room to escape my partying friends.

After that first get-acquainted party the boys and girls moved in on me until most of the rooms on the floor were occupied by my new-found friends and my daily life became just one long party. This was fun at first, but like the little boy with too much candy, it turned into a bellyache and after a week or so I began to look elsewhere for new pleasures.

Chatting with the desk clerk one morning, he informed me that the San Francisco opera was about to begin a new season and that it was excellent. Not knowing what the word "opera" meant, I observed I hadn't eaten it before but would surely like to try a dish if it was as good as he said.

The clerk looked at me for a moment with a funny expression on his face, then burst out laughing. "It's not something to eat," he said, "it's music and fine singing."

He probably retold that incident many times to his friends, who no doubt got a good laugh out of it. One learns word by word the intricacies of a foreign language and sometimes causes a bit of hilarity on the part of the listeners.

Now that I knew what the word "opera" meant, I set off up the street to get a ticket for the evening performance. The lady who handled the tickets was very friendly, and when I mentioned that I had just returned from Alaska and had struck it rich, she informed me that they happened to have an empty box. I wound up with a private box for the entire season.

With the ticket business taken care of, the kind lady reminded me that opera was very high class and that I should come dressed for the occasion. A bit embarrassed at the suggestion, I said I had never, not even in the old country, gone to a show in my underwear.

From the perplexed look on her face, I gathered that I had made another boner in my broken English. Red-faced, I listened to her explanation of what she meant by "dress." To make it even plainer, she showed me a picture of the well-dressed men at the opera wearing long coats and swallow-tails, high hats and fancy pants, such as men wore on the King's birthday at my home in Norway.

Taking my leave of the "lady of the opera," I sallied forth up Market Street, with a slip of paper in my hand telling the location of a fine haberdashery that could supply me with all the necessary clothes and gear for the muscial evening ahead. I was quite satisfied with my morning's adventures. I had learned some more English words, and something about high society.

At the store, the clerks were very helpful and fitted me out with a modern cutaway coat with tails, fancy vest, white gloves and shiny top hat that made me look like the Prince of Denmark. I could hardly wait to get to the opera and show off my finery.

Back at the hotel I spent most of the afternoon dressing in my new outfit and learning to move about in it without being too conspicuous. This was quite a job, especially getting used to that stiff wing collar sticking up under my chin. The knot in the tie gave me no end of trouble at first, trying to get it correct so the ends would be even, but after a couple of dozen tries, I finally mastered that, too.

About 8 o'clock that evening I swept through the lobby to the waiting cab, while bellboys bowed in open-mouthed disbelief at what they saw. They probably remembered my first entry into that same lobby, wearing rags. But if they were astonished or awed, I was nervous and felt about as stiff as a knight of old encased in armor for the first time.

The ride to the opera was a short one, and I was glad of that because the evening fog, with a fine drizzle of rain, was slowly creeping up from the bay and I surely didn't want to get my fine feathers wet the first night out. But if the weather was gloomy outside, it was forgotten the moment I stepped inside the brightly lit entrance to the gathering place of San Francisco's upper crust. The elegance of the crowd nearly took my breath away. Men strutted about like peacocks, their hair slicked down and shiny from pomade. Mustachios that most of them wore were waxed to fine points, some sticking straight out from the upper lip like spears. Others, with even more to do with, had them curled upward, emperor style. They were a sight to behold in the bright lights.

Of course the ladies were much more interesting, with ostrich-plumed hats, narrow waistlines and long skirts sweeping over well-polished floors. Most of them were bedecked with jewelry that glistened in the reflection of the chandeliers and were reeking with various brands of perfume. They must have been loaded with gossip because they kept up a constant chatter, such chatter I had never heard since the fox got into the chicken house back home.

Dazzled by all this glamor and excitement, I was greatly relieved when one of the ushers, with much polite bowing, took me to my private box where I tried to look nonchalant, although underneath I was quite ill at ease in these gilded surroundings.

I am afraid I made quite a stir that first night at the opera, sitting alone in the middle of the box, dressed in all my finery, silk hat on one knee and a big black cigar in my mouth, while all the fine ladies of San Francisco looked me over with their glasses on a stick. Remembering that evening, I think I was the only one smoking in the place, but maybe they were too impressed to throw me out.

Anyway I enjoyed the show and the singing of the hero in knee breeches, who kept hollering how much he loved that big-bosomed dame called Carmen, but personally I think he had poor taste in choosing women.

Back at the hotel it was pure joy to get out of that straight-jacket of a suit and get back to normal once more. I guess I wasn't cut out to be in high society if it meant wearing that kind of togs as a regular costume.

For the next few days after my adventure at the opera, life moved along peacefully, in fact it began to get just a bit too dull to suit me, and that's when I ran into a man selling motorcars.

I had always admired those things chugging along in the streets, and when he suggested that I own one and live according to my means, well, there just wasn't anything else to do but buy one of his automobiles.

It was a thing of beauty, shiny black, with canvas top that could be pulled up in case of rain. It also had big carbide-burning brass lamps in front, and had what some of the fellows at the hotel called a two-lunger engine for power.

I didn't know how to run it myself but the company that I bought the car from supplied me with a chauffeur and all I had to do was to pay the bills. The chauffeur seemed to be a very nice fellow, that is, what I could see of him, for like most of the chauffeurs of that time he was completely encased in linen duster, broad-visored cap, goggles and gauntlets that came halfway up to his elbows. To me, he was a part of the car and could always be depended upon to be parked with this mechanical monster outside the hotel.

Now riding around in the car didn't interest me overly much, for I always liked to walk and had two darned good legs for that purpose, so the car was used mostly by my friends who enjoyed such sports. Most people in San Francisco used horse-drawn cabs.

Motorcars were more or less a novelty indulged in by the rich upon the hill, or by the sporty element.

As the weeks passed, my English improved greatly and I could now order my food from the menu without too many surprises. I could even read the newspapers and make out what it was all about. This I enjoyed very much and at mealtime in the dining room I always had a copy of the newspaper beside me while eating.

I was getting to know San Francisco quite well, so much so that hotel life and the routine of eating, sleeping and generally having a good time began to pale on me. To get away, I began roaming the city during the day from one end to the other and found the waterfront section the most interesting of all. Here I watched the ships from many nations come and go, and occasionally visited aboard some Norwegian freighter where I had a chance to speak my language and hear news from Norway. I usually wound up such a visit by inviting some of the officers and sailors to go with me for a big evening ashore.

All things have to come to an end some time, and my happy days in the big city came to an end rather abruptly. Three months to the day after my arrival I was up early as usual, walking out into morning fog to get my breakfast because the hotel food had become monotonous. Stopping at a tobacco shop to buy some cigars, I discovered that I had only a quarter left in my pockets. Now this wouldn't have bothered me ordinarily, but it suddenly dawned on me that it was all the money I had left in the world. I had paid my weekly bill at the hotel the night before, and that had used up all the money stashed under the mattress in my room.

The situation struck me as rather funny, because I never had learned to worry about anything that fate sent my way. I stood there in the morning chill, tossing that lone quarter around in my hand and pondering what to do next. One thing was sure. I had to find a cheaper place to eat breakfast, and after that I would give some thought to my next move.

Walking down Market Street to the waterfront, I found a small restaurant on the Embarcadero where I got hot cakes and coffee for 20 cents. With the nickel left out of my last quarter, I bought myself a cigar, lit it and strolled back to Market Street.

At the hotel I packed a few things into the old dirty bag that had been sitting in one of the closets. It looked mighty good to me again after I brushed the dust off the weather-beaten material. It was ready for the trail and new adventures.

Knocking on the door of some of my show girl friends, I informed the sleepy-eyed freeloaders that I was now broke and they were on their own. The champagne days were over. Most of them were too stunned at the bad news to say anything at all, but one or two of them offered to lend me money, which I declined with thanks.

I had found 15 cents on my dresser and that was enough to take me across the bay on the ferry. After that, well, the future would take care of itself as usual.

When I checked out at the desk of the hotel, the clerk and the bellboys shook hands with me and one commented with a grin, "When you strike it rich again, we will be here waiting for you."

I had forgotten all about the automobile and the faithful chauffeur, whom I found waiting for me at the curb as usual. The thought of selling the car to raise a few dollars never entered my mind. Instead, I gave the chauffeur all my fine opera clothes and told him to hang on to the car, that maybe I would be back sometime. With a slap on the back, I said good-by to the speechless fellow, swung the pack on my back and headed out of San Francisco with a corncob pipe and 15 cents in my pocket.

On the Bum   14

The road to Seattle turned out to be a long and sometimes a hungry one as I put one foot ahead of the other for some 1,100 miles. The Pacific Highway, as I remember it, was a dirt road graded and graveled near the bigger towns but quite bad in most of the desolate stretches. Still, there were quite a number of adventurous souls traveling over it both ways. I got a few rides with northbound automobiles the first few days, but I soon found out what was wrong with hitchhiking.

Every few miles there would be a flat tire and the repairing of it was quite a time-consuming job; first, jacking up the car, then after much banging with hammer and prying with tire irons, the rim finally would come off. But that was only the beginning. Now the real job was finding the hole, cleaning the rubber tire around it and gluing a patch over the opening. It had to be done with the greatest of care, otherwise the patch would come off in the next few miles and the whole process would have to be repeated.

Being a hitchhiking passenger, I was naturally expected to contribute my labor to this ever-recurring job of patching tires. After a couple of days of this I decided I could make just about as good time walking. From then on I turned my back on all gasoline buggies and let them go chugging by. I caught up and passed some of them, broken down by the roadside.

Occasionally I would ride with some farmer in his horse-drawn wagon. I liked it much better, especially in the late afternoon. Then I usually helped the man feed his cattle or did some other farm chore and wound up with a good supper at a nice family table, a chance to sleep in his barn and a hearty breakfast before departing in the morning.

While it was quite a comedown from my way of life in San Francisco, I found it was easy to adjust myself to the facts of life and didn't mind the change. However, I would not recommend this mode of existence to the younger generation.

From day to day I had not the slightest idea as to where and how I would get my next meal, nor where I would find a place to sleep, but somehow I was fed when I was hungry and come night, if there were not an empty barn or an abandoned shack to crawl into, I simply curled up in my blankets beneath the canopy of stars.

Occasionally I would run into hoboes or "bindle stiffs," as they were commonly called in the West, but these wandering gentlemen as a rule stuck closer to the railroads where the freight trains furnished transportation.

Nearly every railroad town had its hobo jungle where these gentry held out between jobs and trains. Here they cooked up their stew and exchanged news of job opportunities and the low-down on hostile railroad cops to be avoided up and down the line.

They were itinerant workers, not bums. They filled an important place in the labor market as a moving work force for fruit picking, lumber camps and construction jobs. Independent of spirit, most of them would never stick to a job for any great length of time, but would draw their pay on the slightest provocation or, if for no other reason, when they got too "staky." Staky meant they had earned enough to get that rich feeling.

After a trip into the nearest town to enrich the madams, booze peddlers or poker dealers, they hit the road again in search of another job. These fellows were not wholly uneducated and ignorant, many were reasonably well educated, even to a few with college degrees who for various reasons preferred to give up the regulated way of life and lose themselves in the freedom of the road. To me they were an interesting lot, but somewhat out of my line.

90

The days and weeks had slipped by so fast in San Francisco that I had given little thought to the calendar. Each day was pretty much like the one before as I lived in a good-time world. I had hardly realized that summer and fall were long gone until one day snowflakes hit me in the face while I was walking on the Pacific Highway.

Up the road a few miles majestic Mount Shasta stood out, big, bold and ever beautiful against the gray winter sky. Closer, the wind-swept snow flurries across the cracked-up road into the pine forest on each side. It made me feel strangely at home, the snow, the trees and the mountain. I wished I were back in Alaska.

Shortly after dark I entered the little lumber town of Weed, at the foot of the mountain. The town was gaily decorated with lights and greenery. For the first time, I realized it was Christmas Eve.

The wooden sidewalks were jammed with last-minute shoppers and boisterous lumberjacks in town for a holiday spree. I took up with the latter crowd and soon found myself well fed, with a place to sleep in the sawmill bunkhouse and even the promise of a job, after Christmas, from a young logging boss by the name of Murphy. Somebody upstairs was surely looking after this Norwegian.

It was really the nicest Christmas celebration I had experienced in my new country, and the best of food and a real bed for the first time since leaving San Francisco.

When the holidays were over, I went with the rest of the loggers on the train out to the logging camp a few miles from the town. I settled into a four-man bunkhouse that had all the conveniences of home—or nearly so.

It was a new adventure, because it was my first payroll job in America. I made friends with the rough-and-ready loggers, whom I regaled in broken English with tales of my Alaska experiences until they all wanted to go with me, come spring. Even the logging boss would drop into the bunkhouse occasionally, after work, to hear about "digging gold out of gravel and putting it in your pocket." I didn't have the heart to tell them about the times when I nearly starved or froze to death, nor the heartbreaks and disappointments that is a prospector's daily fare.

In a short time everybody in camp knew me as that "Norwegian gold digger," and it proved a big help in my daily work because they all were so willing to help and show me the "how" of things around the logging operations.

My first job in camp was that of a swamper, who chopped off the limbs of a tree, after it had been cut down, to get it ready for the bucker. The bucker sawed the tree into log lengths, which were

91

then hauled into a pile by a heavy steel cable pulled by a donkey engine, and loaded aboard waiting flatcars for the journey to the sawmill.

I enjoyed the work very much and my English improved greatly while conversing with my fellow workers. It was one more wonderful introduction into workaday America, and it made me feel as if I really belonged in the country.

One thing surprised me. I had always heard of California as the land of sunshine and palms, but up here in the northern part of the state, and especially at the foot of Mount Shasta where I worked, we had about two feet of snow. It was never very cold, though, and the logging operation went on all through the winter. It rarely had to shut down because of bad weather.

Camp life was confining and monotonous and most of the loggers spent the evenings in their bunks reading books or magazines. To me, used to living alone in a small log cabin up North, the camp with its commissary, post office, cookhouse and a big dining hall, seemed like a village complete with all the make-up of civiized living.

On an evening I would wander about in the snow, from one bunkhouse to another, visiting the loggers who always gave me a big welcome and plied me with questions about Alaska and opportunities in the territory.

For the first few weeks I enjoyed these nightly visits around the camp, but after a while they began to be boresome, especially on Sunday when there was no work to be done. I couldn't stand being indoors in the smoke-filled bunkhouses while the sun shone brilliantly on the crusty snow and that big white Mount Shasta looked down upon the camp, challenging me to climb it.

Maybe it was my youth or an oversupply of energy that stirred me, but the more I looked at the lofty heights, the more certain I became that I wanted to climb Mount Shasta, or at least get partway up the snowy slopes.

When I mentioned climbing the mountain to the loggers, they promptly told me it had never been done in the winter and that they would have no part in it. In fact, some said, "It might be a good way to commit suicide." That was more than ever a challenge and I decided right there, Mount Shasta or bust.

From a log scaler I borrowed the only pair of skis in camp. On a sunshiny Sunday morning, with a couple of sandwiches tucked away in my pocket, I started from camp toward the foot of the mountain.

Some of my friends stood about on the snow outside the bunkhouses, watching me start on my little adventure. One of them

92

hollered after me good naturedly, "Hey, Norway! Where do you want the remains sent?"

Gliding away on the skis, I had to smile to myself at such a send off. In Alaska nobody saw me and there was nobody to worry about my escapades in the snow, but I had to admit it was nice to have friends.

Above the timber line I found the windblown surface of the snow almost as hard as ice. It was difficult, and in some places almost impossible, to dig the edge of the skis into the snow for a foothold. There was nothing else to do but go home.

In the lee of a hard-packed drift, I ate my sandwiches while enjoying the panorama of the surrounding countryside. Far below in a clearing of the forest, the camp looked like a miniature village, the houses the size of matchboxes and the railroad tracks running into the city of Weed like two tiny black threads on the white snow.

The view was beautiful, but one look at the sun and I knew it was time to start home. I promised myself I would be back another day, all the way to the top. I reached camp at dusk, just as the dinner gong sounded.

It was the second day of March. I had been a hard-working logger for two months now, saving my money for the trip back to Alaska. This time I planned on getting to Fairbanks early enough to travel down the frozen Yukon River on my skis, then up the Koyukuk while the snow was still on the ground. I could travel much faster, carry a bigger load and be at my diggings in time for the spring breakup.

On March 4 I drew my pay, shook hands with the boys and the boss who told me in parting, "There will always be a job whenever you come this way again."

With a "thank you" and a wave of the hand to my friends, I swung aboard the already-moving logging train on the way to Weed and the open road once more.

Now I had a little money in my pocket and could well have bought a ticket to Seattle, but I also had two good legs and a bit of time on my hands, so I decided to continue up the highway and save my money.

Two days of hiking brought me to the top of the Siskiyou Mountains. From there I could look back down on California where the sun was shining, and to the north where Oregon stretched into a white-gray haze. The rainy season was still on, and no doubt it would be raining from there north.

I spent that night in an empty barn a little way beyond Ashland, the southernmost town in Oregon. I suppose I could have gotten a cheap hotel room, but why waste money that I would need so much for the trip North? However, I wished before the night was over that I had stopped in a hotel, for the roof of that old barn leaked like a sieve and kept me on the move from one corner of the place to another trying to stay dry. To make it worse, the old building was infested with huge rats that ran squealing in complaint because I occupied the only dry spot available in the barn.

There was not much sleep to be had that night, and as soon as daylight came I was glad to leave the temporary abode to the rats and get on my way.

It was still raining hard a couple of hours later, when soaking wet I entered a small restaurant in the town of Medford for my breakfast and a chance to dry out. It felt mighty good to get inside out of the rain and the soggy atmosphere that hung like a wet blanket over the countryside.

After the meal I joined several farmers who talked about their crops while they dried their backsides against the potbellied stove in the middle of the room. They were all very friendly to me, although they could not understand why anyone should want to walk all the way to Seattle in the rain. While they were still pondering over this, I bade them good-by and left them by the stove, shaking their collective heads sadly at the poor immigrant who didn't have sense enough to stay in out of the rain.

For the next few days it was just a story of sop-sop-sopping it up the Pacific Highway. Towns came and were left astern, one after another. In Roseburg, Eugene, Salem and Oregon City I paused long enough for a cup of coffee, a plate of beans and a stroll through the main drag to see what excuse the town had for being there.

Finally, one Sunday morning, I entered Portland just in time to hear the church bells ring, calling the "good" to morning worship. As if to celebrate my arrival, the sun came out of the murky clouds, painting trees along the street into a glistening avenue of splendor.

It took me nearly an hour to reach the downtown business section, where Sunday quiet reigned over the almost deserted streets, so quiet I could hear my footsteps resounding on the concrete sidewalks.

I got myself a reasonably clean room in a small hotel near skid row where I would not be too conspicuous in my lumberjack clothes. I had a good suit rolled up in my pack if I should have any use for it, but down in this section of town there were mostly lumberjacks and other transient workers, so there was no sense in bothering to dress up.

The thing I needed most of all was a good bath, for I hadn't had a chance to take one since leaving the lumber camp at Weed 10 days before. At the hotel I found a bathroom down the hall. It was used by anybody having need of it on the entire floor. It was not as elegant as the bathrooms are nowadays. It was an old iron tub with once-white insides that had a shade of gray and plenty of old rings around it, left from previous ablutions. A couple of iron spigots spewed out hot and cold water—cold water almost a certainty. If somebody had taken a bath ahead of you, he had probably used up all the hot water and you had to be satisfied with cold or lukewarm water. Of course, folks were not so fussy about such things those days as they are today, so I got along quite well.

The bath turned out to be fine, with plenty of hot water and a big bar of old-fashioned laundry soap that really scoured the dirt out of my hide and left me smelling as though I had been disinfected.

Moments later, dressed in a clean union suit, (one of those handy ones with a flap in the rear), flannel shirt and logger's pants and jacket, I took off up the street in search of a restaurant. It being Sunday, most of them were closed except for some joints that didn't look very appealing. There was nothing else to do but turn my back upon the "Ptomaine Tommies" of skid row and go back to the hotel and change into some better-looking togs for dining uptown.

At the hotel I dumped the contents of my pack upon the bed and discovered that my good suit was in a sorry shape from dampness and wrinkles. I couldn't wear it until it was pressed. While I was wrestling with this wrinkle problem, the fat little landlady came to my rescue with an iron and an ironing board. I did the job in a hurry, and thanking her, slipped into a clean shirt, collar and a tie—the only outfit salvaged from San Francisco.

Having a flair for the finest when in the money, I went to the best hotel in Portland, the Multnomah, and blew myself to a four-bit dinner in the hotel dining room, with a 10-cent tip for the waiter.

After dinner I strolled about the business section for a while, trying to make up my mind whether to go to church or to a show.

The only church I could find was a mission half filled with down-and-outers waiting for a free meal at the end of the sermon, and I surely didn't belong there. A little farther along I passed the Salvation Army having an outdoor meeting on a street corner. I lingered there for a few moments, listening to them, then strolled on up the street.

I was about ready to call it a day and go back to the hotel when the blinking lights of a vaudeville theater on Broadway caught my eye. For 15 cents I got a seat down front where I had a close-up view of the magician performing on the stage, the cuties doing tricks on abbreviated bicycles and the comedian cracking jokes that I mostly couldn't understand. Anyway, it was a pleasant evening and a much-needed rest from pounding the highway.

I had intended to spend only one day in the City of Roses, but I was so tired that I slept nearly the clock around and it was too late in the afternoon to check out by the time I woke up. However, things like that didn't worry me. It only gave me another evening in the big town and a chance to get better acquainted with Portland.

On April 4, I landed in Seattle, raring to go North. I got a chance to work my way to Alaska aboard the steamer *Northwestern,* an opportunity that I gladly accepted, for it would save me quite a bit of money that I sorely needed for a grubstake.

The ship wasn't scheduled to leave for another week, and during this waiting period I ran into an unexpected windfall that earned me $100 in a matter of minutes.

It happened on the same day that I got my job on the ship. I had been working all day, helping to stow cargo for the trip North, and after supper aboard ship I took a swing around the city just to pass the time.

Drifting along on the poorly lighted street, I watched a sailor in uniform zigzagging between the buildings and the curbstone just a little way ahead of me. He was evidently loaded to the gills and only a good pair of sea legs kept him from going down.

He was no concern of mine and I was just about to turn around and go back the way I had come, when suddenly out of the shadows two hoodlums jumped him. The poor sailor was too drunk to defend himself and went down in a heap with the two on top of him, trying to get his wallet or other valuables he might have.

Being well-used to making quick decisions in Alaska, where my life might depend on quick thought and action, I ran to help the guy the only way I knew—with my fists. One of the tough guys squared off to stop me from interfering, but the next moment he was flat on his back on the sidewalk, dead to the world. The other hood disappeared into a nearby alley.

People gathered around, helping the sailor to his feet and making sure he still had his money. A stocky, fat-faced man with a cigar on one side of his mouth grabbed me by the arm and excitedly inquired, "What you got in them hands, boy? Dynamite?"

I wanted to get on my way now that all was well again, but the stranger insisted on talking to me away from the crowd, and suggested that we step into a nearby restaurant. I had nothing to lose, so we slipped away from the group that was watching the hoodlum slowly getting to his feet, spitting blood and holding his busted jaw.

Over a cup of coffee the stocky man with the cigar informed me that he was a fight manager, and that he needed a substitute middleweight for that same week.

"Would you like to fight in the arena, six rounds for $100?" he asked.

Not being familiar with the fight game, I didn't understand the situation too well, but after much explanation I got the main idea. He wanted me to fight somebody at the sports arena, Crystal Pool. For the job I would receive $100 win, lose or draw.

The money was too much of a temptation to turn down, and before we parted company I promised I would show up at the gym the following evening to get the hang of the manly art of boxing.

Back aboard the ship, the boys kidded me plenty, but they all promised they would be around for the fight.

The next two evenings after work, I went to the gym to work out in preparation for the fight. Some of the crew came along, mostly out of curiosity, I suppose, but they assured me afterwards that what they saw impressed them and they thought I had a good chance to win the fight. Personally, I could see only that $100 bill, but I would surely do my best to make it an interesting evening for the spectators.

On the night of the fight I arrived with my seafaring followers about 20 minutes before fight time, to find the arena packed to capacity with a popcorn-eating, foot-stamping crowd, eager to see some luckless gladiator thrown to the lions. It made me disgusted to look at them, but it was too late to change my mind now.

The dressing room was a madhouse, with the manager and trainers running around trying to fit me into a pair of borrowed trunks and shoes, while from the arena came the noise of the crowd whistling and clapping to get the show under way.

Things moved fast once I got into my trunks and had the gloves fastened on. Before I hardly realized it, I was sitting on the stool in my corner of the ring. In the opposite corner my opponent climbed through the ropes amid much clapping and cheering by the customers, who evidently held him in high esteem. He was a swarthy fellow, swathed in a bathrobe with a towel over his head and a battle-scarred, ugly-looking face.

Besides my trunks, I only had on a ragged, paint-spattered sweater belonging to one of my sailor friends, with the inscription "SS Northwestern" in front.

The entire arena was blue with smoke from cigars and cigarettes which hung like a haze in the bright light over the ring. It was a strange environment indeed, the noisy crowd, the lights and my manager and seconds all giving me advice at the same time. It was a new experience that fascinated me, although I would just as soon have been a spectator.

I didn't feel any fear of my opponent, but had that same feeling I knew from Alaska when I was in a tight spot, to act fast with a clear head.

The referee called us to the middle of the ring for instructions, then we went back to our corners where seconds pulled off sweaters. The bell rang for round one, and I was on my own.

My opponent came tearing out of his corner like an Alaska bear. My instinct warned me to keep away from his swinging paws and wait for a good opening. I soon learned that I knew nothing about boxing. Every time I got close, he bopped me on the nose and danced away before I could touch him.

This soon made him overconfident. When he came in for another swing at my face, I ducked and landed a solid punch with all my weight behind it, square on the point of his jaw. Before he had a chance to recover, I followed it up with blow after blow to face and body. He crumbled on the floor just as the bell rang for the end of the round.

That turn of events seemed to please the crowd greatly, because they cheered wildly. In front of me the manager told me over and over to rush in and finish him off before he could recover.

At the beginning of the second round he tore into me again, but I could feel the steam had gone out of his punches and he didn't worry me any more. From my corner they kept hollering to finish him off, but somehow I didn't have the heart to hurt him unnecessarily. To me it was poor sportsmanship. As you see, I didn't know much about fighting for money.

All through rounds two and three I pulled my punches, taking a lot of snappy clouts in return and not realizing that he was fast coming out of the doldrums, getting stronger all the time.

My corner urged me to knock him out in round four, before he got another chance at me, but I dismissed the warning and went into the ring intending to play along until the end of the fight. That

98

was where I learned a most important lesson, to protect myself at all times.

We met in the middle of the ring, sparring and occasionally swinging at one another, until suddenly he let go with a haymaker that caught me on the left side of the face and sent me spinning to the deck. He had gotten his strength back and wasn't playing the game my way at all.

With my head dancing, I jumped to my feet. The referee cleaned the rosin from my gloves and motioned for the fight to continue. I was so woozy I could hardly see my opponent moving in to finish me off. For a few seconds I ducked and backed away to clear my head.

Then my big chance came. In his eagerness to knock me out, my opponent rushed at me wide open. I caught him with a solid right to the jaw, then kept pounding his body and face alternately until he collapsed.

The referee held up my arm in token of victory and the crowd cheered, but I was glad the thing was over. I had quite enough prize fighting.

After sitting through the rest of the fights, "the man with the cigar," my manager for the night, gave me the $100 he had promised. Then he took me and a couple of my sailor friends to a nearby restaurant for a steak dinner. His kindness was suspect, because during dinner he tried to get me to sign a contract that he just happened to have in his pocket. The contract would have made him my manager for all future fights.

I declined the offer with thanks, but just to make sure he would pay for the steaks, I mentioned casually that if I should change my mind upon returning from Alaska in the fall I would sure look him up. We shook hands on it and the sailors and I took off for the ship.

Back to the Diggings 15

I was Alaska bound again, not as a paying passenger this time but as a hard-working member of the crew. Perhaps it was just as well, too, for it might teach me the value of money, something I should have learned long ago or I wouldn't be broke now.

Over my shoulder I saw Seattle glistening in the bright noonday sun while I bent my back with the rest of the boys, heaving in the dripping wet hawsers used for mooring lines. At least I was on my way again, and next time I would surely do better and hang on to my money. I had learned my lesson—or so I thought.

Puget Sound lay like a mirror ahead of the ship's bow, reflecting the timber-clad hills and projecting points in the calm waters, where fishermen trolling for salmon gave us a friendly wave in passing.

An incoming sternwheeler ferry from Bremerton saluted us with a toot of the whistle, its passengers lining the rail for a look at the ship northbound for Alaska.

By the time we hard-working sailors had coiled up the mooring lines and got things shipshape generally, Seattle was far behind us, leaving only snow-capped Mount Rainier visible above the haze.

Life aboard ship quickly settled down into the routine of eating, sleeping and enjoying the scenery unfolding along the shore of Puget Sound and the Inside Passage, a panorama of beauty such as can only be found one other place on earth—the coast of Norway.

Our first stop was Ketchikan, where we spent most of a day unloading supplies, then on to a couple of smaller ports. We continued to Juneau, where we stayed overnight, unloading most of our freight. From there we steamed westward to Cordova and Valdez. At Valdez I got off the ship to take the wagon trail up to Fairbanks.

The captain gave me $15 for my work on the way North, and a couple of old blankets. He also told me I could have all the grub I could carry from the ship's stores. By the time I had had my pack stuffed and ready for the trail, I had given him a lesson in packing. I staggered away with about 150 pounds.

Happy to be on solid ground again, I made my way over the planking of the old dock. With a last glance at the ship and a wave of my hand in good-by to the crew, I was on my way again.

Getting back to the claim was just a case of walking and walking more, until my legs ached from the trail and my back ached from the heavy load.

It took more than two weeks to reach Fairbanks, where I found the population much bigger than the town, so much so it was impossible to get a room in any of the tiny hotels there. The price of food was sky-high, too, even higher than in Nome the previous year. But my luck was good. I got a job helping an old prospector build sluice boxes and other equipment in preparation for his summer work, slept in his little cabin and had all the food I could eat.

I was glad to get that opportunity, because it would be several weeks yet before the ice went out of the rivers. I made arrangements to go down the Yukon by boat, to reach the claim a much easier way than going in by Nome.

Fairbanks was a much bigger town than I had expected and a very exciting one, filled with people from all over the States and many foreign countries. Walking down the muddy street, one could hear the languages of Scandinavians, Germans, Slavs and a few French-Canadians, all jumbled up together. Now all of them were in a hurry to get their outfits together for their diggings or prospecting trips farther on, and the main thoroughfare was a bedlam of activity.

My English had improved so much that I was able to converse with people and make all my wants understood. By talking to the fellows acquainted with the country, I learned much about the mining camps out of Fairbanks and along the Yukon River.

From studying the map, I had laid out a route that would take me in the general direction of my diggings, and I hoped by taking the shortcut to save much valuable time.

Finally, after much waiting that really had me champing at the bit, the ice went out of the rivers and we were ready to start down the Yukon. I had gathered the essentials for a summer trip. I expected to be back in Fairbanks by fall, for I had no wish to get caught over winter again. Just how I would get back I didn't know at the time, but as long as there were boats on the river, I figured there would be no trouble getting transportation.

On a pleasant sunny morning we were ready to start down the Chena and into the Tanana on our way to the Yukon. The boat, a nondescript tub, was run by a kerosene engine that had to be heated with a blowtorch before it would start. But, once it got going, we made fairly good speed down the river swollen by the spring thaw.

There were six of us aboard when we left Fairbanks, including the owner, a fellow by the name of Galt who, according to my fellow passengers, was married to an Indian woman and lived somewhere along the lower Yukon.

Galt spent most of his summers freighting the rivers for miners, trappers and trading post operators. Like many boat owners of that day, he played an important part in the summer transportation on the Yukon River.

Before gold was discovered in this vast territory, it had only a handful of whites making their living trapping, fur buying or trading with the Indians. They cry of gold changed all this and brought on a stampeding horde of greenhorns like myself, clawing their way through the territory and raping the land of its riches. But such is our so-called civilization, "enlightened" yet so destructive.

For hours at a time I sat on a box beside Galt, listening to tales of his early years in Alaska while he deftly steered the boat around deadheads and debris floating down the river. Only the chug-chugging of the kerosene engine broke the afternoon stillness.

In Fairbanks people had referred to Galt's boat as the "petroleum boat" and now I saw the reason. The short stovepipe sticking up from the engine emitted not only the most perfect smoke rings I have ever seen, but left a bluish haze astern that reeked with the smell of kerosene.

The four other men in the boat must have had quite a celebration before leaving Fairbanks because they slept soundly, heads resting against bags of flour and beans, with hats down over their faces shielding them from the bright sunlight, oblivious to the world around them.

"Had to drag them away from a poker game," Galt observed, nodding his head toward the sleeping men.

The journey down the Tanana was most interesting. This part of Alaska was new to me and quite different from the bleak, barren land around Nome. There seemed to be a lot of activity along the shorelines, with small boats moving about. Smoke from cabins half hidden in the brush rose into the blue sky overhead.

We stopped in a couple of villages beside the river, not because we wanted to visit with the Natives but for Galt to do some tinkering with the engine that had an occasional coughing spell and wanted to quit. I guess it was nothing serious, although each time I could hear him muttering something about "that damned dirty coal oil." After a little work with the screwdriver and pliers, he had the thing chugging away once more.

It took us several days to reach the town of Tanana on the Yukon River, where we unloaded some supplies before proceeding. We found the Yukon much harder to navigate. Its current, increased by the high water and drifting logs, became a real menace to our boat.

We passed a number of Indian camps where we saw the Natives with their families putting up salmon for the winter. Their sled dogs greeted us with a chorus of barking as we passed by. To me it was a revelation. I had not seen any Indians the year before, but then I had been farther north and inland from the rivers.

It was daylight all through the night now. I didn't keep track of the days, but I think it was about a week since we started out. The boat got into a bit of trouble that caused me to change my plans somewhat. As it cruised along close to the north shore of the river, the propeller hit a submerged log, which put it completely out of commission. There was nothing else to do but get it up on a beach to survey the damage.

Lucky for us, we found a small river or creek emptying into the Yukon. Pushing and shoving with a pair of oars and a long boat hook, we managed to get the boat into the shallow water, pushing it astern upon a sand bar where the propeller would be out of the water so we could work on it.

Once the stern was out of the water and secured, we gathered around to have a look at the damage. There was plenty of that. The propeller blades were twisted out of shape and useless. To us it seemed the end of the journey, but not so to Galt. It must have been an old story to him because he didn't seem perturbed at all. He bit off a fresh chew of tobacco, then with hammer and chisel set about to drive the cotter pin out of the shaft. It would have been an easy job except that the shaft and the propeller had been together so long that it had turned into a glob of rust, defying the efforts of our simple tools.

The five of us stood around helplessly, watching Galt work on the problem. He shooed us off when we wanted to volunteer our mechanical skill.

"This is one job I must do myself," he grunted, while cutting and chiseling away at the stubborn pin.

It took him about five hours to get the thing off, and in the meantime some of the fellows had caught a couple of salmon and had them frying in a pan over the fire. At least we would eat while waiting for the verdict as to what we should do next.

103

Galt didn't mention that he had any spare propellers aboard. I suppose he took it for granted that we knew. After stuffing away all the salmon he could hold, he nonchalantly opened a box in the back of the boat and brought out a shiny new propeller. While we watched in open-mouthed surprise, he proceeded to fit it onto the shaft.

To the five others, it was a great relief to know they would shortly be on their way again downriver. As far as I was concerned, this would be the end of the boat ride.

While Galt was working on the propeller I had studied the map and discovered that the creek where we were tied up ran straight north in the general direction of my claim. Now if I could follow the stream northward, instead of going away around up the Koyukuk, I would be able to save a great deal of time. It surely was worth trying.

When I mentioned my plans to the other fellows, they promptly reminded me that it was my life and if I wanted to commit suicide it was my privilege. Old Galt was noncommital, but mentioned that he probably would be coming by this sand bar a number of times during the summer. He would keep a lookout for me, in case I changed my mind and returned to the Yukon.

I got my pack together ready for the long trail north. About midnight we had some cold salmon and coffee. Before leaving I helped shove the boat back into the water, and waved good-by to my friends who chugged away into the Yukon.

Shouldering my pack I started up the creek, following close to the shoreline so I wouldn't get lost. In the next 20 miles or so I passed a

number of Indian
camps along the creek,
but most of them had sled
dogs running loose so I gave
them a wide berth by walking around their camps, always coming back to the creek again to get my bearings.

The Indian population stayed mostly along the bigger rivers and inlets where the fishing was good. As I got farther into the Interior, I left them behind. However, there was plenty of life around about me, but not of the human kind. There were fur-bearing animals of all kinds, such as foxes, martens and many others that were unfamiliar to me.

Walking along the creek, I intruded on many a bear family living high on salmon, most of them giving me only a passing glance and continuing with their business of catching fish. Only one, that I took to be a grizzly because of his immense size and the grayish-colored hair along the flanks, disputed my passage for a few minutes. This one stood up on his haunches, pawing the air with his forepaws and talking to me in a low growl. I stood my ground and he soon went about his business, too.

The country I was traveling through was covered with a sparse growth of scrub timber with little or no underbrush, so I could see for quite a distance ahead at all times. The trees were mostly a type of black spruce with a few birches and aspens. The stony ground had a rich dark-green covering of moss that I imagine made good grazing for caribou, of which I saw plenty.

Having neither watch nor calendar to mark the days, I had lost all track of time. The days were swallowed one into another with hardly any distinction, since daylight remained all through the night. But such things didn't worry me. I slept when tired and ate when hungry. Only one thing bothered me—what if I should not be able to find my claim again?

But that too was quickly dismissed from my mind. I just had to. I had not seen a human being since leaving the Indian camps, then one day I discovered post holes dug in the gravel bed along a creek. Someone had been testing the ground for gold and I knew there were prospectors around, not far away because the holes were freshly dug.

Walking along a couple of miles farther, I came upon two of the prospectors panning beside the creek. My first thought was to rush up and speak to them, but having developed the wariness of the wild, I decided against it.

I knew that if the prospectors had had no luck there, they would probably follow me farther north, and I surely didn't want any company at my diggings. After studying them for a few moments from among the trees where they couldn't see me, I continued on my way.

For about two weeks I followed the creek until it took a sharp turn eastward. Here I left the creek behind and continued over a long row of hills, until on the other side of a divide I came to another creek running westward, no doubt eventually into the Koyukuk.

The country began to look strangely familiar. That evening I came to the place where I had met the Swedes on my way out the previous year. Happily, I made camp to rest a bit and have a look around, for now I knew where I was.

The Swedes' cabin was still in good shape and a couple of their sluice boxes were neatly turned upside down beside the creek, but there was no sign that they had been there recently. Evidently their pay streak had run out and they had gone elsewhere to try their luck.

It was pleasant to stay overnight on their old campground and cook my supper over the ashes of their old campfire, while memory went back over the past year and a half. Grinning to myself over the coffee cup, I recalled the excitement of my own struggle, my success and the wild days in San Francisco—and here I was, to try it again!

My Hole in the Ground   16

After a good night's sleep by the Swedes' old diggings, I set out for my hole in the ground. Following the landmarks and blazes on the trees, I arrived at my claim late in the evening of the fourth day. I found the old sluice box with the tools and gear underneath just as I had left it the year before.

The snow was all gone now except for patches here and there on the shady side of the hills. The creek was high with water, running over the banks in places.

It was with strange emotions that I set up my camp and enjoyed my evening pipe by my own campfire once more. I had that same wonderful feeling of being free again. Only the rustling of the wind in the trees and the soft gurgling of the waters in the creek broke the stillness of the subarctic spring night.

This was living, away from the regimented herds of so-called civilization, away from where human beings like ants followed the leaders blindly in their daily appointed tasks or starved if they failed to fit in with the wishes of the masters.

Now I don't want to contradict the Good Book, that part about earning bread by the sweat of your brow. That is certainly the everlasting truth. I sweat plenty, shoveling gravel into my sluice box for 16 hours a day or more. It was not for the love of money, because I knew I couldn't hang on to it and didn't particularly care. Yet, here I was back again, ready to face any hardship that might come my way, to dig more of the yellow stuff out of the ground.

"For what?" I asked myself. The answer would not come. Anyway, the coffeepot was empty by this time, so I gave up my philosophizing for the evening, rolled into my blankets and slept like one at peace with the world.

I was up early the next morning but found high water above the pay streak in the gravel bed. I had to content myself with preliminary work. But, there was plenty of that to be done. First I had to move the sluice box down to the water's edge and get it ready for operating. Then it was necessary to channel the water so it would run over the frozen gravel and help thaw it out. All of this consumed a great deal of time and it was several days before I was ready to start sluicing.

By noon of the fourth day I had all my equipment set up and the sluice box in position to begin operation on the pay streak, or rather the continuation of the pay streak that I had worked the previous year.

It was refreshing to be able to use my muscles again, to take the kinks out of my somewhat stiff body that had become too used to the living of civilization. Of course all the walking up the trail had taken care of my legs, but there is nothing better for the back, shoulders and arms than shoveling gravel into the box for 16 hours a day or longer. At first it feels as if it will kill you for sure. You ache until you groan out loud, and when you have finished the day, it is a great effort just to lift the coffee cup to your lips. But it has its compensations. After a while your body becomes tough, your shoulder and arm muscles bulge and you have that wonderful feeling of confidence in your strength. You could lick a grizzly bear barehanded.

So the days went by in a happy routine of working, eating, sleeping, and most interesting of all, the weekly cleanup of the sluice box. It showed that I was still in the pay streak, adding to the poke that was filling fast with nuggets and dust.

I took time off from my work occasionally to catch some graylings in the creek, where they swam in such schools it would have made a fisherman's enthusiasm mount to the heights. The abundance of fish also brought company to my camp, a rolling fat mama bear and her two rollicking cubs.

I had just turned in for the night when I saw them coming down the creek toward my sluice box. The mama walked sedately along the creekbank while the young ones dashed in and out of the creek, splashing the water like two happy kids on an outing. It must have been close to midnight, for the sun had long since gone down, but it was still daylight and I could watch my visitors capering about my diggings.

They came within about 100 feet of where I lay on my blankets, when suddenly mama got my scent and reared up on her hind legs, sniffing the air and pawing like a boxer with her forelegs. She turned slowly from side to side to get a look at the intruder in her domain. The young ones, sensing something was wrong, stayed close behind the mama bear, imitating her belligerent attitude by getting up on their fat little hind legs, only to fall over backwards like two butterballs.

I had to change my position on the blankets, and she spotted me turning over on my elbow. With a ferocious launch, she got down on all fours and came for me. She made four or five steps with her mouth wide open, showing flecks of white slobber around her jaws.

My right hand instinctively reached for the rifle beside me, although I knew I would never use it unless it was a case of saving my life.

The two cubs in the meantime were back at their play and had found a new fascinating game for themselves, that of balancing themselves on the narrow edge of the sluice box until one of them fell off and got stuck inside the narrow box. Squealing like a pig and wriggling frantically to get out of the contraption, he made mama bear forget all about me.

She surveyed the situation for a moment, then with a swoop of her paw she scooped the cub out of the box with such force that he landed with a splash in the creek.

Gathering her brood with grunts and paw, she stood on her haunches facing me in a last warning as if to say, "Don't you dare get any closer."

I didn't. I just stayed there on my blankets, watching until the happy little family ambled off down the creek.

The show over for the night, one tired Norwegian snuggled into the blankets, dreaming of bears and such.

I had no worries about food, for there was plenty of game to be had anytime my taste should run to caribou or bear. For the time being I lived mostly on fish, beans and an occasional strip of bacon that I had brought along. After that I would try to live as much as I could off the land, saving what little flour I had left for special pancake breakfasts when in the mood for something different.

One day I had a funny experience cooking rice for the first time. An experienced cook knows that rice expands, but I discovered it the hard way. I poured the entire bag, about five pounds, into my cook pot. It came to within an inch of the top of the pot, then I poured in water to well above the rice and set it on the fire to cook.

It kept boiling and expanding, constantly rising to the top of the pot with me frantically dipping the stuff into every vessel I had, until even the gold pan was full of it by the time it was done. That week I lived on rice, morning, noon and night. But, so we learn by trial and error the little secrets of life.

Since my return to the claim the weather had been beautiful, just cool enough to enjoy hard work, with sunshine most of the time. I worked stripped to the waist and my body took a rich tan from wind and sun.

It was too much to expect such weather all summer in Alaska. Toward the end of June I awoke one morning in wind-driven rain beating down on my blankets, soaking me thoroughly before I found shelter under a spruce. At first I thought it was only a shower, but it got worse as the day wore on, bringing with it a cold clammy fog that hung over the forest in a gloomy pall.

The rain continued for nearly a week. I couldn't afford to waste the time so I worked with water dripping down my face, with clothes sticking to my body, and my boots soggy inside and out. It wasn't exactly pleasant, but the rain had its good points, too. It helped thaw some of the gravel, which made digging a great deal easier.

Each night I built a huge campfire out of spruce logs that burned even in the rain, and dried my clothes after a fashion before crawling into the blankets.

All things have an end and so did the rainy week. That rain brought to life a swarm of mosquitoes that plagued me for the rest of the summer. They got so bad I had to leave my shirt on while working. I fashioned a headband out of an old shirt, with strips of cloth hanging down over my shoulders to keep them off my neck. But I suppose I had no kick coming; they were the natives and I the visitor.

That weekend I cleaned up the sluice box and found that the rain had indeed been good to me. There was more than twice as much gold in the box as I had found in any previous cleanup. Among the nuggets and dust was one rough-looking chunk that weighed well over a pound, the largest nugget I had taken out of the ground so far. That one I kept in my pocket for luck.

For several weeks the weather held good and my riches increased. Then one day something happened that upset me. I had company, that I knew, but not who nor how far away. The discovery stirred mixed emotions in my mind. When you prospect alone, and especially while working a pay streak, you become alert and suspicious of strangers horning in on you.

While shoveling gravel into the sluice box, I noticed white chips of wood coming downstream and going into the sluice box. It could mean only one thing—somebody was working the creek somewhere above me. Since the water was clear and showed no sign of mud, I knew they either must be quite a distance upstream, or else they had not yet started sluicing.

I couldn't work any more until I found the answer. Fortified with a cup of coffee and a couple of cold pancakes, I slung the rifle over my shoulder and set off upstream in search of my neighbors, whoever they might be.

Following the winding creekbed through the thin scattered forest, my eyes were alert for ax marks on the trees and other indications of human beings. By late afternoon I had covered about 15 miles without finding any sign of where the chips might have come from. I would have kept on going but since I had brought no food with me, I gave up for the time being and returned to my camp.

I knew there would be no rest or peace of mind until I could find the source of those innocent little chips that came dancing down the stream, announcing the arrival of newcomers into what I, by this time, considered my own domain. After a restless night, with dreams of bandits who stole my gold and all kinds of crazy things, I was up by the time the sun was two hours high, perhaps 5 o'clock.

This time I took along food for a couple of days, a blanket and my rifle. Not knowing what kind of folks would be around now, before leaving I buried my gold under the campfire and threw a few pieces of fresh wood on top to burn into a natural ash heap.

Traveling fast, I reached the turning point of the previous day about noon and stopped for a bite to eat before going farther. The sun was pleasantly warm, and after eating my meager lunch I stretched out on an old windfall log to rest and enjoy my pipe.

Tired from the long walk, I soon dozed off with the pipe in my mouth. I don't know how long I had lain there when the crackling of dry brush nearby brought me out of my sleep with a start. Thinking perhaps it was a bear, I cocked the rifle and slid down beside the log where I could have a view of my surroundings without being seen by whatever or whoever was approaching.

I didn't have long to wait. Moving slowly up the slope toward me was a tall, lean whiskery-faced individual that I recognized immediately. It was one of the Swedes, the one called Axel, in whose camp I had stopped overnight on my way out the previous year.

I just couldn't resist having a little fun with him. I waited, hidden by the log, until he came closer, then yelled at the top of my voice, "Hey, Axel!"

The words echoed through the forest. The Swede stopped dead in his tracks, as if had been struck by lightning. The expression on his face was so funny that I burst out laughing and he spotted me crouching beside the log.

For a moment he looked puzzled, no doubt wondering who I could be calling his name here in the wilderness. Then as he slowly advanced, his bewhiskered face turned into a grin of recognition.

"You scared the devil out of me, Norske," he laughed, rushing up to shake my hand in greeting. Then the two of us sat down on a log to have a little powwow.

He was very curious to find out what happened to me in the States since we met, and I was equally interested in finding out what he was doing in my neck of the woods.

Since I was host on the log, I didn't waste any time in telling him all about my San Francisco trip, about all the pretty girls, the opera, my motorcar and all those nightly parties in my hotel where champagne ran like water in the spring thaw. I never drank any of the stuff myself, but Axel, who liked to play around with Old Man Bacchus occasionally, had his tongue hanging out just thinking about the champagne.

With my story told, Axel regaled me with tales about himself and the Finn, who had spent the winter in Seattle living high on the hog until most of the summer's earnings had dribbled away.

Carlson, who was married and more settled, had bought a small farm near Salem, Oregon, and was in the business of raising prunes. His wife took care of the place while he was away making more capital for the venture.

Subconsciously, the conversation registered with me. It was a plain picture of a smart man saving his hard-earned money and the jackasses throwing their wealth to the winds. With a bit of pain, I secretly had to admit that I had been one of the latter. Oh well, I would soon have another chance to find out if the lesson had taught me something of value.

Axel had been out hunting meat when I met him but now that could wait, for as he said, "It isn't every day we have visitors out here in the wilderness."

The gangling Swede led the way to their camp. His two companions, Carlson and the Finn, were busy shoveling gravel into sluice boxes. Both of them promptly threw the shovels onto the gravel bar and came toward me in friendly greetings. Then they set about getting a feast together for their guest.

I spent the afternoon and night visiting with my friends and it was a most enjoyable break, indeed, from my lonely existence.

They had moved their camp from where I had met them the year before and were working a pay streak here on the upper end of my creek. They, like me, were rushing the work and planning to hit the trail for the Outside and Seattle by early September.

Meeting them also solved my problem of getting to Fairbanks in the fall. They had made arrangements for a boat to pick them up on the Yukon, and invited me to go along. This was surely a break, for lately I had given much thought as to how I would get back to civilization, come fall.

Early the next morning, with a hearty breakfast under my belt, I took leave of the Swedes and the Finn and set out for my own camp, which I reached just before sundown.

Time was getting short. Soon the subarctic fall would be upon me with frosty nights and generally bad weather, a forerunner of that long cold winter. It made me shudder just to think about it.

Swinging the pick with renewed energy, I dug and shoveled the gravel into my ever hungry sluice box. I watched the muck go dancing through the box and gush out the other end. The heavier gold should be settling behind the riffles to enrich me on cleanup day.

One thing I was learning to my dismay: the pay streak was getting thinner and thinner the farther I dug, a sure indication that it would run out before long. But it didn't matter much, I told myself, for I had made a good summer's haul and after this trip I would settle down. I dreamed of a business, a wife and a home where I could sit back and laugh at these adventurous years. But, I guess I still had a lot to learn.

Back to the Bright Lights

I knew it must be well along in August because the mosquitoes had left for the season and it grew dark early in the evening. The stars and moon came out again for the first time since spring. The nights also became quite chilly, another reminder for me to hurry, hurry, hurry with whatever had to be done before freezeup.

The pay streak had come to an end and I was post-hole prospecting along the creekbank in the hope of finding another streak. However, I wasn't kicking, I had done very well in the short summer and was now satisfied to retire to a better life.

I had almost given up waiting for my friends, when late one evening Carlson, Axel and the Finn came into my camp. It was cloudy and dark but I could hear them stumbling along over the rocky terrain, Axel swearing in Swedish, long before they came into the light of my campfire. Each unshaven, long-haired giant carried a pack big enough for a mule.

"Got anything to eat, boy?" Carlson grunted, dropping his heavy pack on the ground. Then half to himself, "I couldn't have made it another mile with this load. I think Axel put rocks in my pack."

"That's just what I suspected you did to me," Axel laughed. "Those last few miles took all the sap out of me, too."

The Finn dropped his load and with a nod at his companions, commented to me, "You know, Norske, what I think is the matter with those two guys? They spent too much time playing around Seattle and I have had to nurse them around all summer, trying to get some work out of them."

They were all in a jovial mood, chiding each other while I cooked some man-sized caribou steaks over the fire.

I had already had my supper, so while they ate I cleared out my sluice box by the light of the campfire. There was not much in it, mostly fine flakes and a couple of bean-sized nuggets, and I knew it was the end of my pay dirt. It didn't worry me.

With the work all done and my things packed, we settled down to talk around the campfire. It turned out to be one of those rare evenings of comradeship on the trail that lingers on in the memory. The mellow odor of fresh-made coffee and strong pipe tobacco hanging in the air added a nice atmosphere to the friendly chatter. Even the taciturn Finn was in a fine mood, playing his harmonica.

Time after time the coffeepot was passed around the circle and pipes refilled until Carlson broke the spell with the comment, "It will be a long hard day tomorrow, fellows. Maybe we had better hit the sack."

To this we all agreed, and as a fitting end to a perfect evening, the melancholy howl of a wolf came from out of the distance, followed by the stillness of the Alaska night. The dying campfire and the twinkling stars kept watch over four snoring, blanket-wrapped men.

For the next seven days we traveled Indian fashion, in single file toward Carlson's rendezvous with the boat on the Yukon River. He told us he knew the country well, but as we traveled along behind him, we sometimes wondered just how well. He led us over a rugged terrain where all the valleys and canyons seemed to run east and west while we tried to keep a southerly course. We waded across more creeks than I thought existed in all Alaska, and they kept us soaking wet up to armpits most of the time.

But Carlson, and his little pocket compass that he constantly consulted, proved to be right. On the evening of the seventh day, just about sundown, we landed on the bank of the sluggish Yukon.

There was no boat in sight, but after we had made camp for the night we saw a faint light that we took to be from a lantern. A little later we noticed a small campfire about half a mile upstream from us. It was too late to investigate who our neighbors might be, and anyway we were dog-tired and hungry from the journey. So we set about cooking some caribou meat for supper and drying our soggy clothes by the fire.

I guess we would have made quite a picture to an outsider, the four of us sitting around the campfire dressed only in our underwear and chewing on chunks of meat.

Before we were ready to turn in for the night, the full moon came up over the hills, turning the landscape and the river into a painter's dream with streamers of silver dancing about over the restless waters. We were too tired to enjoy the scenery, though, and one by one tumbled off to sleep.

We awoke the next morning to the barking of dogs. Peeking up from under the blanket I discovered we had company, two husky dogs that barked at us and wagged their tails at the same time, and three long-haired Indian kids looking us over with much curiosity. They kept their distance at first, no doubt wondering whether it was safe to come closer, but when Carlson struck his head out from under the blankets and greeted each one by name, they all broke into a toothy grin of recognition. They had come to inform us that the boat would be ready to take us across the river and on to Fairbanks about noontime.

After breakfast we followed the kids to their cabin home on the edge of a little creek running into the Yukon, and were introduced to our boatman and his family. To my surprise, the boatman's name was Kjelson. He was a countryman of mine who, as a young man, had been shipwrecked near the mouth of the Yukon. Making his way upriver, he met and became partners with an old trapper until the old man died.

Kjelson liked the country because it was so much like his native land. Later he married an Indian girl and settled down on the Yukon, trapping and trading with Indian friends who trusted him implicitly.

I judged the man to be about 60 and the wife near the 50 mark. Each had a ready smile and a sense of humor that made the visit a very pleasant one.

After a noonday meal together we said good-by to this happy family and set out for Tanana and Fairbanks.

The 20-foot boat was piled high with furs, bundles of blankets and other supplies until it looked like a seagoing haystack moving upstream against the current. We didn't make much headway when the wind was against us, for the tiny marine engine spit and coughed until we thought the nuts and bolts would pop right out of it, but we overcame that obstacle by staying close to the shoreline and made the crossing when the wind changed in our favor.

The trip was quite uneventful. After two tedious weeks we finally arrived in Fairbanks with our precious cargo. Here we paid the boatman, Kjelson, and the four of us with packs on our backs started off down the trail to Valdez in a happy mood.

The Valdez trail at that time was little more than a footpath worn over rocks and dirt by thousands of miners' feet. Here and there through the years it had been enlarged with ax and shovel to make it more passable for packhorses and later on for freight-laden wagons.

We, like most miners, used our own two legs for transportation, stumbling along over rocks and ruts with our heavy packs until our bodies ached and our legs were ready to cave in. Although we stopped frequently to rest, we made fairly good time and reached Valdez in slightly less than two weeks.

It sounds easy, telling about it now, but looking back I remember spending a couple of days in Valdez when I could hardly walk from blisters and red spots on heels and toes. At that, I was much better off than Carlson, who got blood poisoning in a toe from nails sticking inside one of his boots. He had to spend days in two-by-four hospital while waiting for a ship to Seattle.

There was a ship leaving for the Outside the very day we arrived in Valdez, but every available space was sold out and there was no chance of our getting passage. We had to simmer down and be content to wait and hope for space on the next one.

We were lucky to get a room with four cots at a small frame house that had been turned into a hotel. Here my three companions and invited friends spent most of the days and late into the night playing poker.

In fact, for this reason our room became so popular that I could hardly get to my cot for a little sleep until the early morning hours when the game finally would break up. Being a young man with no particular interest in card games, I imagine I was rather a pain in the neck to my friends in this respect, as they were to me with their constant and lengthy poker sessions. But, rooms were hard to get and at least this was a place to rest and kill time between games.

I spent most of my daytime hours around the waterfront, watching the activities there and hoping to get reservations on some ship to the Outside. After two weeks of waiting, my vigil paid off. I managed to get passage for the four of us on an old rusty hulk of a ship that if my memory serves me right was called the *North Star.* She had been up to Nome, and for some reason or other had her schedule changed to make stops at Seward, Valdez and Juneau.

There were four empty bunks left open for the run south and I lost no time in securing them for myself and my friends. The mate

116

informed me that she would be leaving within the hour, and after completing the transaction I tore off up the street to inform my friends of the glad tidings.

At the hotel the poker game came to a sudden end. The boys dropped the cards and gathered up their money and belongings in a mad rush to get to the ship and claim their accommodations.

It was high time, too, for when we arrived at the dock the ship's whistle blew for departure and there were a number of men waiting for our bunks in case we didn't make it on time. Some of these fellows were so anxious to get Outside they offered several times the price of our tickets to change places with us.

While we were packing away our gear the ship cast off, and when we got back on deck Valdez was slowly fading in our wake.

The Regimented World   18

From the bow of the ship I watched the city of Seattle rise out of the mist like a rain-washed pearl in the morning sunshine, the bright sun reflecting from a thousand windowpanes on the hillsides.

Other passengers joined me, leaning on the rail and admiring the splendor of the view. One of them, who evidently had been around, called it, "Istanbul of Puget Sound."

Now I couldn't say about that, never having visited the Bosporus, but looking at Seattle from the deck of an incoming ship, it is a place of great beauty and fortunate are those who call it home.

Nosing our way through the oily slick water toward our own particular berth, I heard church bells ringing from somewhere on the hill ahead and realized for the first time it was Sunday. The workaday hustling harbor was quiet, and the ships tied up along the docks lay in the serene peace of the Sabbath.

The passengers who had been lazing about the ship for the past week or more suddenly came to life. Lugging bags and suitcases, they gathered on the shore side of the deck, all ready for a hurried landing once the ship was moored.

Usually there were a lot of people on the dock when an Alaska ship came in, but we must have been unscheduled because there were only a few stevedores waiting to take the lines, and the usual hustle and bustle of arrival was completely missing. Not that we cared about such things, we were in Seattle, the only thing that mattered.

As soon as the gangplank was out the four of us, packs on our backs, trouped ashore and headed up the deserted street toward Pioneer Square, our hobnail boots resounding on the concrete sidewalks in the still morning air.

Here and there folks on the way to church turned to look at the four goldminers, and I guess we were quite a sight with our windburned faces adorned with dirty-looking whiskers and hair that had eluded the barber's shears for much too long. But in spite of the outward appearance, we were probably the happiest men in town that morning, for in our packs we carried enough gold to insure leisurely living for some time to come.

At the hotel just off Pioneer Square, where I had checked my suitcase the previous spring, we were given a royal welcome. The hotel personnel, well used to the free-spending Alaska crowd, catered to our every wish with a happy smile.

After we had registered for our rooms, the clerk called the hotel barber, who came after church to attend to our tonsorial needs. While he worked on us he had the window blinds drawn, because Seattle at that time had a law against doing business on Sunday. We paid him well, however, for his trouble and he seemed more than glad to take the chance.

The housekeeper ironed the wrinkles out of my only suit, badly in need of such services after being packed away for so long. The bellboy polished my shoes until I could see my face in them, and supplied me with a brand-new necktie to complete the change into a gentleman.

Before putting on all the finery, I took care of the most necessary job of all, that of soaking Alaska out of my dirty hide with much hot water and plenty of soapsuds. Believe me, you can never fully appreciate a hot bath until you have gone through a similar experience.

The task of getting into my dress shirt and suit proved to be quite an undertaking, after using nothing but comfortable clothing for so long. The white silk shirt that had fit so well in San Francisco the year before now stuck to me like a plaster, and the fancy wing collar poked me under the chin every time I moved my head.

Whether I had gained weight up North or it was just bulging shoulder muscles developed from shoveling gravel, my fine

118

tailor-made suit fitted me about two sizes too soon and made me feel like a stuffed hot dog. There was nothing to do about it, though, until the stores opened on Monday.

It was past noon and my stomach was growling for attention. I set off for Carlson's room down the hall. He was all dressed up, too, only his clothes fitted him much better than mine. Across his vest he wore a heavy watch chain made of gold nuggets, very popular with goldminers of that day.

Carlson was sort of a straight-laced fellow who didn't believe in spending his money on booze and wild women, that is, beyond a certain point. I being a nondrinker also, we hit it off well together and decided to find the best eating place in town for a real dinner and maybe a show afterwards for dessert.

They say that everybody has a vice of some kind and if that is so, mine must be eating. When in the money, there is nothing I like better than good food and good company.

On the way out, we stepped in to see how Axel and Finn were getting along and found them whooping it up with whiskey and a couple of damsels in the room, so we quietly beat a retreat and left them to their own design.

Carlson and I had a seven-course dinner at a famous restaurant on Seneca Street, after which we took in a show at the Orpheum Theater. After the show we ambled around the city looking in the well-lighted store windows. This may not seem much of a homecoming celebration, but to a man who has spent months in the wilderness it is a wonderful change just to mingle with the sidewalk crowd and listen to their happy chatter. It gives you a feeling of belonging and being a part of things.

About midnight we were back at the hotel. I hurried to my room to get out of the straight-jacket suit and stiff collar that by this time had me blue in the face from strangulation. It took an hour of pacing the floor and exercising to get the blood back into proper circulation again. One thing was sure, I would have to buy some new togs first thing in the morning.

Monday morning, with my pockets full of money, I felt like I wanted to buy everything in sight, much to the delight of salespeople in the stores along the way. Suits and coats, shirts and all the other finery that go into the making of a dude were packed in boxes and delivered to the hotel until I didn't have room for any more.

Now I was dressed up with the best of my civilized brethren, but looking at myself in the mirror I still had two distinct features that set me apart. My face and neck, burned to a dark tan from wind and weather, and a pair of tough-looking oversized hands at the end of fancy sleeves somehow didn't fit in with the rest of the elegance. But I was secretly pleased with that difference, for I had earned my wealth the hard way.

At noon I met Mrs. Carlson at the hotel. She had come up from the prune farm at Salem to pilot her husband safely through the pitfalls of the big city that lay in wait for Alaska miners.

She was a good-looking gal in a buxom sort of way, with a heavy Swedish accent and a positive way of expressing herself that left little doubt as to who was the boss of that family. Carlson himself was a changed man with the arrival of his better half. Instead of the roughneck I had known in Alaska, he was now a very domesticated husband with an ever ready "Yes, Dear."

In a way I envied him. To have someone look after you and keep you in the straight and narrow might not be bad at all. On second thought, no, no. It could be disasterous to a man's freedom, and that I valued above all else. Perish such thoughts!

The Carlsons were leaving on the afternoon train for Portland. We had a last dinner together in the hotel dining room. Axel and Finn were there too, bleary eyed and beaten from an all-night bout with Bacchus but otherwise on their best behavior. To Axel it was an especially trying hour, for having spent most of his adult life working in logging and mining camps, his English had become a bit tarnished. In fact, he had become so proficient in the dubious art of cursing that almost every sentence was punctuated with a damn or worse. Now in front of Mrs. Carlson he really had to watch his speech, and I saw him swallow hard, choking down a couple of choice outbursts.

After dinner we took the two Carlsons to the train to see them off for Oregon. Mrs. Carlson made me promise that I would visit them in the land of prunes—and as an afterthought, she reminded me with a grin, "There are lots of fine girls down our way that would make you a good wife."

The departure of the train began the breaking up of the four of us, friends of the trail, for Finn had just informed me that he was leaving for New York and the old country in the morning. Axel had many friends in Seattle and would probably be hanging around, spending his hard-earned money on whiskey and women, and when broke by spring, would head for Alaska again.

As for myself, I couldn't decide whether to go down to San Francisco and continue where I left off making a jackass of myself, or go east to some city in that area. However, events of the past year had made me a bit more mature, or maybe it was age creeping up on me. At any rate, I couldn't make up my mind just yet.

We left Finn at the railroad station where he had some business, and Axel and I walked up the street until we came to a joint on First Avenue where a back-room poker game was in session. Here I shook hands with the rambunctious Swede and never saw him again.

During the next three days I spent most of the time getting acquainted with Seattle and the more I saw of it, the better I liked it. If only I could get into some kind of business while in the money, I surely would be happy to make this city my permanent home. But, the only business that I knew anything about was gold mining, and I had had no training for anything else.

This good sense, uppermost in my mind at the moment, had a fierce competetor nagging in the back of my head. Why don't you raise whoopee for a while, have a good time, you are young only once, remember the fun in San Francisco? So while the days went by, the two schools of thought fought for control of my brain and my pocketbook. Like a small boy with a dime, gaping at the tempting display of a candy store window, should I blow it now or put it in the piggy bank?

On the evening of the third day I decided on a compromise. I would make a train trip to New York, see the Statue of Liberty again, and maybe fate would take a hand. Just to make sure I was doing the right thing, I stopped in front of a store window on First Avenue, dug a coin out of my pocket and flipped it. Heads for New York, tails for a big blow in San Francisco. San Francisco won out and I felt that I had been fair and square to myself. San Francisco it would be in the morning.

For the next two days I played tourist, enjoying the long train ride down through Washington, Oregon and finally into California. The panorama from my big car window was beautiful but not of course to be compared to that of Alaska. I was already getting partial to the Great Land.

About noon of the second day the train crossed into California and shortly thereafter glistening white Mount Shasta came into view, a silhouette against the blue sky. An early season's snow reached down into the timber line, below which was the logging camp near Weed where I had spent a couple of happy months the previous spring, laboring for a grubstake.

So many things had happened in the past two years. I had been rich, had my fling, then that long hungry walk back to Seattle and north to Alaska for more gold.

Now traveling in style again, I leaned back in that comfortable chair seat, grinning to myself while puffing on my after-lunch cigar and watching the green pine forest that reached into the distance toward the mighty mountain. This was living and I rather liked the feeling of being rich again.

Late that evening we reached San Francisco. With a bit of anticipation I entered the portals of the Palace Hotel, thinking I should see some of the people I had known the year before. But there was not a familiar face, no one to rush out and shake my hand this time. I guess they were to familiar with those 30-day millionaires who came, had their big days and passed on into oblivion as far as the hotel was concerned.

This time one room with bath was sufficient. My appetite for parties had vanished. I felt I had become an American, able to speak English enough to get along well and to read the daily papers without any trouble.

There was one man I was anxious to see again, the fellow who acted as my chauffeur and in whose care I had left my Cadillac. I really did not expect to find him, thinking he would have taken off for parts unknown, enjoying the fancy buggy he had inherited.

To my pleasant surprise, upon stepping outside the hotel the very first morning in the city, there was my Cadillac parked at the curb exactly as I had left it. At the wheel, dressed in the regalia of diverse gold braid that I had bestowed upon him, was my chauffeur. On the side of the car there was a sign that read, "Limousine for Hire."

For a few moments I just stood there flabbergasted, taking in the situation. I didn't know what to say. Maybe we were in the taxi business together.

The chauffeur had been studying me too. He suddenly jumped out of the car and rushed up to me with an air of uncertain expectancy, obviously wondering whether I would take kindly to the idea of the limousine being used for a taxi during my absence.

The situation called for a conference over a cup of coffee and some Palace French pastry. For the next hour we talked and laughed while I got the low-down on the limousine business. It had prospered for over a year and had brought in considerable money. My share had been put away in the bank in my name!

The more we talked, the more I appreciated my scrupulously honest business partner and decided to let things stand the way they were. After all, it would be nice to have a growing bank account waiting for me in case of a streak of hard luck in the North.

Funny thing, here I had a partner whose name I had long since forgotten if indeed I ever knew. It was rather embarrassing to have to ask him again, but he confessed with a wide grin that the name of his half of our company was Ingvar Davidsen. That was a common Scandinavian name but it must have been away back because he appeared to be a typical San Franciscan, a native son.

For the next few days I made a number of trips around the city in "our limousine." I went out to Golden Gate Park to have a look at the *Gjoa*, a little wooden 89-foot sailing sloop, the only ship (up to that time) to conquer the Northwest Passage around the top of the North American continent. This voyage was under the command of the famous Arctic explorer, Roald Amundsen, who later became the first man to reach the South Pole. I knew that ship very well, for she had been in the shipyards in my hometown, Tromso, undergoing preparation for the voyage.

Ingvar was a born businessman and kept that buggy of ours on the go every day. The hotel management was glad to have him around to drive the affluent trade to business appointments during the day and to the nightspots for entertainment in the evening hours. I rode along in the front seat on some of these excursions, but found it dull and boring to watch our mostly drunk patrons having an imaginary good time spending their money.

Some changes within me had taken place since my last hilarious visit to San Francisco. Was I growing up? Or had Alaska taken such a grip upon me that the pleasures of the big town had faded out of my system? I could not answer this question in my mind but one thing was sure, I had soured on large cities. After five days I packed my suitcase, said good-by to Ingvar and the limousine, and took a bus up the coast to Eureka.

The bus, a converted Pierce Arrow seven-passenger touring car, was quite comfortable although a bit crowded and dragging on the springs with seven persons inside and a collection of baggage on top. But it was pleasant to be on the go again. I especially looked forward to see the giant redwoods in the north coastal regions of the state.

The journey to Eureka was uneventful, although the roads were nothing to brag about. The road was full of chuckholes that swayed the old Pierce Arrow like a drunk, and the passengers had to grab for something to hang on to every few minutes. From Santa Rosa north it had been raining all night and our car soon looked like it had been dragged through a mudhole. A cleaning apparatus rigged on the windshield was operated by the driver by turning a little crank back and forth. Whenever the goo got too thick and the visibility zero, the driver gave the handle a couple of licks which cleaned the windshield sufficiently to enable him to see enough to stay on the trail. Luckily there was very little traffic. In the northern part of the state the road dwindled down into a simple dirt lane with turnouts to let oncoming traffic pass.

About midnight we arrived at Eureka. Some of my fellow passengers had been there before so I followed them up the dimly lighted street to a three-story wooden hotel, the Vance, where most of us spent the night.

The next morning I discovered Eureka to be rather a pleasant little lumber town with an ever present perfume of fresh-cut lumber hanging in the air. Across the inlet from the city schooners were loading lumber to be transported mostly to San Francisco, with an occasional larger ship taking on cargo for Japan.

I spent several days inhaling the ozone of the redwoods and getting acquainted with diverse loggers, mill workers and the native population. The loggers, except for the married local people, were mostly made up of drifters who worked the logging camps of California, Oregon and Washington until they had made a stake.

I ran into such a fellow one morning in a saloon. He had gathered about all the money he could use for the time being and had decided to take off for Portland.

There wouldn't be much adventure in just going up to Portland, but after having a look at the car that he had just bought for the magnificent sum of $50, I agreed with him it could be quite exciting.

While the owner was inside the bar taking leave of his logging camp pals, I had a second look at the four-wheel bargain. A sign in white chalk on the side of the car read, "Portland or Bust." Walking around it for a closer inspection, I felt the latter could be very much of a possibility.

The doors on either side were hanging loosely on rusted hinges supported with wire. The starboard side showed signs of having had a hard brush with some immovable object. The radiator had an empty tomato can for a cap and a considerable drip-drip of water was going on underneath the car.

I started to lift the hood for a look at the engine. It came off and landed on the road with a bang. This brought the owner out of the saloon to see who was tampering with his purchase, and he appeared to be quite well fortified for most any journey.

He seemed like a happy-go-lucky fellow, laughing and joking with the bystanders assembled to watch his departure. He informed the world in general he was taking off for Portland. "Would anybody care to go along?"

Well, I hadn't thought of it before but here was a challenge for an adventure of a different sort and it intrigued me. I didn't have much time to make up my mind because he already had his hand on the crank. When I mentioned that I might be willing to risk my life, too, in this great adventure, he just waved his free hand and chortled, "Hop in, friend." With that, the engine sprang into action.

We stopped long enough at the hotel to pay my bill and grab my suitcase, then chugged out the main street, Portland bound.

The logger's name was Charley. He had served a hitch in the Navy and was a bit afraid they would call him back in. The war in Europe had been going on for three years now with no victory for either side. We agreed that President Wilson was doing a good job in keeping us out of the mess, but there were many voices advocating our entry into the war on the side of England and France. I said I would just as soon stay out of any entanglements in Europe. Having been brought up there, I had learned much about the petty jealousies among those nations.

We pulled into the village of Trinidad with our radiator steaming, which it did every 30 miles or so. Trinidad had a whaling station, a small outfit and probably the only one in America in operation at that time. Being Norwegian, I had to stick my head in the gate and ran smack into a man by the name of Fredriksen who was boss of the place. He had learned the whaling business in my hometown and knew almost everybody there so it developed into a sort of a reunion.

We were just leaving the station when outside the gate we met four very well-dressed people. The men wore knickers, short pants that came to an end at the knee, with fancy wool stockings on their legs and sporty-looking shoes. The ladies were high society for sure, with their long dresses and big wide-brimmed hats fastened down with miniature fishnets.

One of the two men asked if they could go inside and I called Fredriksen, who took them in tow. When they came out they thanked me for helping them, and one of the men handed me his card. It read: Cornelius Vanderbilt. I handed the card to my partner, who glanced at it for a moment and threw it away contemptuously.

On our way again, and nearing the little town of Gold Beach at the mouth of the Rogue River, the engine or something connected to it began giving out horrifying noises. It wasn't a groan or a squeak but a combination of both, and on top of that a banging noise came from underneath of the automobile.

Charley, with his ears cocked to the sound, commented, "It's just the way of the Model T's. They are all alike, noisy but reliable."

About that time the car came to a stop, the radiator steaming until the tomato can danced. The engine still ran, though. There was no stopping it, even with the switch off.

"What did I tell you," said Charley, easing himself out the door, "reliable to the end."

Outside the car he stood for a moment, hand on chin studying the situation. The south end of the engine was resting on the ground, separated from the drive shaft, but like a miracle, still running.

Surveying the situation, we agreed that it needed some minor repair work to get it all together again, and now was the time to begin the project.

Occasionally other travelers came by and some of them stopped to watch my mechanical genius of a partner do a complete rebuilding job right in the middle of the street.

First the engine had to be raised to the original level of the frame. This was accomplished with a post taken from a farmer's fence and used as a pry. When we got the engine high enough, he hung on to the pole because he weighed the most and I tied the engine and shaft in place with a rope and a piece of chain that someone threw us.

The radiator hose had broken off, but that problem was solved with a rubber tube from an old milking machine I found in a deserted barn near by.

By this time the onlookers were cheering us on, and a couple of salesmen in a shiny new Ford placed bets with each other on the success of the undertaking.

After a couple of hours of hard work came the big moment. Would it run? Charley took charge of the crank and instructed me how to wiggle the dohickey on the wheel to keep the gas flow and spark working together. It was a tense moment, everybody standing by, craning their necks not to miss anything. Charley gave a mighty heave on the crank and the engine came to life with a roar. Our audience cheered and we felt quite proud. Lucky there was water in the nearby ditch for the radiator.

In Gold Beach a blacksmith welded the broken frame together and it held without any further adventures until we reached Portland.

Turning into a filling station for what we hoped would be the last water stop, Charley hit the curb a little too hard. With a bang the engine landed upon the sidewalk, completely separated from the rest of the car.

The station operator came over, and grinning at the sign on the side, commented, "Well, you made it, wherever you came from. Give you five bucks for the wreck."

126

"Sold," said Charley, pocketing the bill.

Moments later two weary travelers, lugging their belongings and laughing, headed downtown for the Multnomah Hotel.

For a few days I enjoyed the hospitality of the Multnomah Hotel, with excellent food and a fine bed to sleep in. But boredom crept in once again. This kind of life was not for me.

Standing at the entrance of the hotel, I saw the sidewalk parade each morning as the good citizens of Portland rushed to work to earn their daily bread by 10 hours of industrial or office slavery, six days a week for the magnificent sum of $2 or $3 a day. At that the wages had almost doubled since my arrival in the States. The war in Europe had made more jobs available, especially in the shipyards and war-related industries.

The fingers in my coat pocket touched a roll of bills bigger than what most of these people made in a lifetime. I felt sorry for them and their way of existence.

Maybe while I was in Portland I should drop in on Carlson and his wife. It would be interesting to see how they raised prunes down Willamette county way. Salem was only about an hour's train run from Portland. I walked to the station and took the Shasta Limited south. I expected to stay only overnight so I didn't bother taking a bag, and kept my room in the hotel until my return.

In Salem a sleepy "jitney" driver waiting at the curb for business said he knew where that Alaska guy named Carlson lived, and for four bits would take me there.

It was a beautiful drive and I really couldn't blame Carlson for retiring into such pleasant surroundings. Well-tended orchards lined the road on either side of the shiny hard blacktop road. I had walked through this town before on my way to Seattle and had gone through on the train to California, but this was the heartland never seen from main highways nor trains.

Carlson looked up from pruning a tree to see who was getting out of a taxi in front of his house, and that was the end of work that day. Seemingly overjoyed to see me, he called to his wife. She came out of the kitchen wiping her hands on her apron and grinning from ear to ear as she approached me.

For the next two days Carlson and I talked Alaska every chance we had to be alone. But Mrs. Carlson had called in some of her neighborhood friends to help celebrate the event, and among them was a very attractive blonde that Mrs. Carlson insisted would make a lone prospector a very fine wife. Eighty acres across the road were for sale, just the thing, she suggested, for a young man to get a good start in the prune business.

127

I must say I had a couple of most interesting days in the prune country, but by the end of the second day I suddenly remembered that I had some business in Seattle to be taken care of right away. Mrs. Carlson was a fast worker as a matchmaker, and Helga the blonde one appeared to be cooperative. Being very green in this particular game, I thought I had better get out of there and head for the wilderness while I was still free.

I was in Seattle by evening. I had plenty of money left, but now I knew where I belonged.

Two days later, on a drizzly February morning, I watched from the afterdeck of the freighter *Latouche* as the city of Seattle faded into the gloom astern. I was Alaska bound.